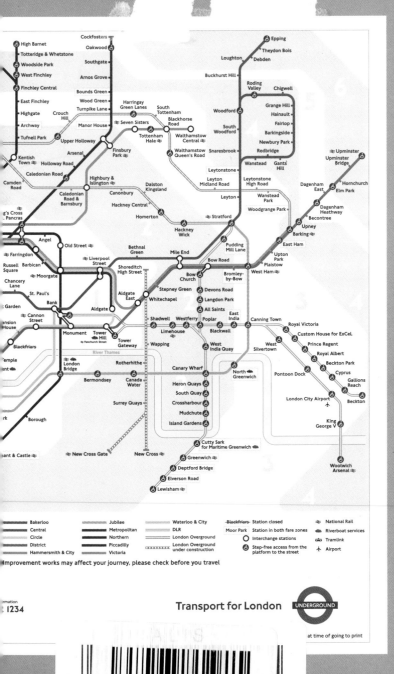

Bakerloo
Central
Circle
District
Hammersmith & City

Jubilee
Metropolitan
Northern
Piccadilly
Victoria

Waterloo & City
DLR
London Overground
London Overground
under construction

Blackfriars Station closed
Moor Park Station in both fare zones
○ Interchange stations
Step-free access from the
platform to the street

National Rail
Riverboat services
Tramlink
Airport

Improvement works may affect your journey, please check before you travel

Transport for London

UNDERGROUND

at time of going to print

D0243489

London

Author: Robin Barton
Verifier: Robin Barton
Managing Editor: David Popey
Project Management: Bookwork Creative Associates Ltd
Designers: Liz Baldin of Bookwork Creative Associates Ltd and Andrew Milne
Picture Library Manager: Ian Little
Picture Research: Liz Allen, Alice Earle, Carol Walker and Michelle Aylott
Cartography provided by the Mapping Services Department of AA Publishing
Copy Editors: Marilynne Lanng of Bookwork and Pamela Stagg
Internal Repro and Image Manipulation: Neil Smith
Production: Rachel Davis

Produced by AA Publishing
© AA Media Limited 2007
Reprinted 2008
Updated and revised 2010

Published by AA Publishing (a trading name of AA Media Limited, whose registered office is Fanum
House, Basing View, Basingstoke, Hampshire RG21 4EA; registered number 06112600).

 This product includes mapping data licensed from the Ordnance Survey®
with the permission of the Controller of Her Majesty's Stationery Office.
© Crown Copyright 2011. All rights reserved. Licence number 100021153.

ISBN 978-0-7495-6688-3
978-0-7495-6701-9 (SS)

A CIP catalogue record for this book is available from the British Library.

The contents of this book are believed correct at the time of printing. Nevertheless, the publishers
cannot be held responsible for any errors or omissions or for changes in the details given in this
book or for the consequences of any reliance on the information it provides. This does not affect
your statutory rights. We have tried to ensure accuracy in this book, but things do change and we
would be grateful if readers would advise us of any inaccuracies they may encounter.

We have taken all reasonable steps to ensure that the walks and cycle rides in this book are safe
and achievable by people with a realistic level of fitness. However, all outdoor activities involve a
degree ofrisk and the publishers accept no responsibility for any injuries caused to readers while
following these walks and cycle rides. For advice on walking and cycling in safety, see pages 16–17.

Some of the walks and cycle routes may appear in other AA books

Visit AA Publishing at theAA.com/shop

Printed and bound in China by C&C

A04393

CONTENTS

■ HOUSES OF PARLIAMENT

Welcome to...
London

London: a city of black cabs, red buses, Beefeaters and Horse Guards. True, but there's so much more to this dynamic place. To truly experience Britain's capital to the full you need to live like a local, not a tourist. This book will guide you through London's major sites and introduce the less well-known attractions that may be new to even long-term residents.

In such a resolutely urban landscape, it is still possible to join an evening bat-spotting walk or hear the bark of red deer. London's green spaces are a haven from the crowded streets and there are sporting facilities aplenty.

London's shopping is second to none. Make it your business to seek out the enticing boutiques of Notting Hill, the delicatessens of Marylebone and even the grand outfitters of Mayfair. The markets are also must-sees.

Cultural life encompasses opera, theatre, cinema, street festivals, art exhibitions and much more. The South Bank and the Barbican are arty hot spots; you can enjoy summer concerts too. Do leave time for some of the world-class museums and galleries – they've had years to perfect their act! What's more, most are free, with late-night openings as well.

ESSENTIAL SIGHTS

London is different for everyone and your own list of the top things to visit and the best things to do will depend entirely on how you like to spend your time. However, unarguably, at least one of the capital's world-class museums will come near the top of anyone's list. The opportunities for shopping are unrivalled as are the range and quality of the city's restaurants and art galleries. For those who want to escape the crowds, there are several large parks where you can walk, rollerblade or even hire a boat.

1 South Bank
London's revitalised riverside incorporates many of the city's leading cultural venues including the British Film Institute and the Southbank Centre. There are incomparable views across the river and essential sightseeing from the London Eye.

2 Shopping
Everyone has heard of Oxford Street, and its stores are certainly geared up for the crowds that visit daily. You will want to go to Knightsbridge for Harrods and Harvey Nichols, too. But do explore other areas of the city – each has its own range of stores, shops, boutiques and markets.

3 Museums
London's museums cover natural history, science, history, arts and crafts, childhood and much more. Most of them have been established for years and have huge collections.

4 Covent Garden
This bustling indoor market area is surrounded by streets of smart shops. A variety of performers entertain the crowds.

5 The Parks
London's green spaces offer activities and events as well as being wonderful places to relax, play, walk and picnic.

6 Art
London has a wide range of art galleries, as well as superb public art and statues. This is the Regency Room at the National Portrait Gallery.

7 Pop culture
Shoreditch – a mecca for the creatively minded.

8 Pubs and restaurants
Britain's capital has some of the world's best restaurants and chefs. In the last 25 years or so, they have transformed the eating habits and expectations of the nation. Most world cuisines are on offer in London today.

9 Events
London's cultural calendar reflects both its diverse population and centuries-old history. Ceremonies, such as the Changing of the Guard, and sporting extravaganzas meet vivacious, exotic events such as the annual Baishakhi Mela in Brick Lane. Year-round, events give a glimpse of another world within the city.

10 Architecture
The newest buildings in London showcase the skills of the world-class architects such as Norman Foster whose modern designs, such as the glass-and-steel City Hall, stand alongside some venerable buildings from the past.

6

7

8

9

10

DAY ONE

For many people a weekend break in a vibrant city is a popular way of spending their leisure time. These four pages offer a loosely planned itinerary designed to ensure that you make the most of your stay, whatever the weather, and enjoy the very best that London has to offer.

Friday Night

You should check into a city-centre hotel for two reasons: first, London's nightlife will be on your doorstep, so expensive late-night taxi rides won't be required, and second, you will always have plenty of transport options to choose from over the weekend. You will find several good, mid-priced hotels in Bloomsbury, which is close to the British Museum.

Saturday Morning

Have a light breakfast at the hotel before heading to Southwark to browse around Borough Market. Saturday morning is probably the busiest time to visit this thriving farmers' market, but half of the fun is watching London's ever-expanding army of amateur gourmets shopping for the finest olives, breads and cheeses in the 18th-century marketplace. The area is often used to film period dramas and nearby back streets beckon the more inquisitive shopper.

Saturday Lunch

For lunch, you can graze from the tempting food stalls at Borough Market or have a Spanish-style snack at Tapas Brindisa, which is one of the best tapas bars in London.

Saturday Afternoon

After lunch, head for the South Bank and take a spin on the London Eye. You should book in advance to minimise queuing, but the wait is worth it for the aerial views of the capital. Then cross Westminster Bridge for a tour of the Houses of Parliament, which is open only in the summer months. At other times of the year you'll have to settle for seeing the outside of the Gothic Revival building on a boat trip departing from Westminster Bridge. Families will enjoy the aquatic life in the London Aquarium, a wet-weather option situated close to the London Eye.

Saturday Night

Find out what a gastropub can cook up at the renowned Anchor & Hope on the Cut, between Southwark and Waterloo tube stations. Get there in time for a pre- or post-show meal. A short way down the river is Shakespeare's Globe theatre; it is an open-air space, so be sure that the weather is fine. During the winter months, have a night out at one of the South Bank's excellent venues: the National Theatre, the National Film Theatre and the Royal Festival Hall among others.

BOROUGH MARKET

REGENT'S PARK

DAY TWO

Your second and final day starts with breakfast in Marylebone. Don't linger here too long, because next you'll head to nearby Regent's Park and visit London Zoo or just see what is happening in the park. After lunch, you can decide whether to go to Little Venice or Hampstead.

Sunday Morning

Start the day with a hearty breakfast and a browse through the Sunday papers at a café in Marylebone, such as Villandry. Then cross over Marylebone Road into Regent's Park. Even in this 24-hour city, Sunday morning remains a relaxed time and you can watch Londoners at play on the park's sports pitches. Refresh your senses with a stroll around the finest rose gardens in the capital or go boating on the lake. London Zoo is in the north corner of Regent's Park and the site is in the process of undertaking a number of interesting conservation projects.

Sunday Lunch

You could head up to Manchester Square to take in the glorious works of art from the 18th and 19th centuries on display at The Wallace Collection. After this have lunch at the museum's brasserie restaurant, The Wallace. Alternatively, stay in Regent's Park for a simple but tasty lunch at the pretty Garden Café.

Sunday Afternoon

From Regent's Park you have two main options. You can head off west along Marylebone Road to Little Venice, close to Paddington station. From here you can take a narrowboat along the canal – now cleaned and restored – to Camden Lock. In Camden, Sunday afternoon can be spent scouring the shops and stalls at the Camden Market and the Stables Market for some funky accessories and vintage clothes. The alternative is to travel north from Regent's Park on the tube to Hampstead, a Georgian village overlooking central London. Houses once occupied by Freud and Keats are open to the public and Kenwood House on the Heath is a wonderful place to explore. There are guided walks around this corner of London, including a tour of Highgate with the Original London Walks company, or you can do your own thing and explore the oldest section of fascinating Highgate Cemetery. If you have time, return to your central hotel via the trendy eateries of Farringdon and Clerkenwell, on the fringes of the City, where London's workers will return to the business of making money for their paymasters on Monday morning.

MINIMUM TIME The time stated for completing each route is the estimated minimum time that a reasonably fit family group of walkers or cyclists would take to complete the circuit. This does not allow for rest or refreshment stops.

MAP Each route is shown on a map. However, some detail is lost because of the restrictions imposed by scale, so for this reason, we recommend that you use the maps in conjunction with an AA Street by Street map. These are available in both sheet map and atlas format.

START This indicates the start location, normally a tube station. The six-figure grid reference is prefixed by two letters showing which 62.5-mile (100km) square of the National Grid it refers to. You'll find more information on grid references on most Ordnance Survey maps.

CYCLE HIRE We list, within reason, the nearest cycle hire shop/centre.

❶ Here we highlight any potential difficulties or dangers along the cycle ride or walk. If a particular route is suitable for older, fitter children we say so here. Also, we give guidelines of a route's suitability for younger children: for example the symbol 8+ indicates that the route can probably be attempted by children aged 8 and above.

Walks & Cycle Rides

Each walk and cycle ride has a panel giving information for the walker and cyclist, including the distance, terrain, nature of the roads and paths, and the nearest tube station.

WALKING

All of the walks are suitable for families, but less experienced family groups, especially those with younger children, should try the shorter walks. Route-finding is usually straightforward, but the maps are for guidance only and we recommend that you always take the relevant AA Street by Street map with you.

Risks

Although each walk has been researched with a view to minimising any risks, no walk can be considered to be completely free from risk. Walking in the outdoors will always require a degree of common sense and judgement to ensure that it is as safe as possible, especially for young children.
• Some sections of route are by, or cross, busy roads. Remember, traffic is a danger, especially in the busy streets of the capital.
• Be prepared for the consequences of changes in the weather and check the forecast before you set out.
• Ensure the whole family is properly equipped, wearing suitable clothing and a good pair of boots or sturdy walking shoes. Take waterproof clothing with you.
• Remember the weather can change quickly at any time of the year. In summer, take account of the heat and sun by wearing a hat, sunscreen and drinking enough water.

CYCLING

In devising the cycle rides in this guide, every effort has been made to use designated cycle paths or traffic-free riverside routes, but inevitably there are some busy on-road sections where you may prefer to dismount.

Rules of the road
• Ride in single file on narrow and busy roads.
• Be alert, look and listen for traffic, especially on narrow lanes and blind bends, and be extra careful when descending steep hills, as loose gravel or a poor road surface can lead to accidents.
• In wet weather make sure that you keep an appropriate distance between you and other riders.

- Make sure you indicate your intentions clearly.
- Brush up on *The Highway Code* before venturing out onto the road.

Tips for urban cycling

- Don't undertake lorries or buses in stationary or slow-moving traffic; vehicles may be turning left. This is the most common cause of accidents in the capital.
- At junctions, use the advance stop line for cyclists if available. Ensure lorry drivers can see you.
- Use cycle paths and lanes wherever possible. Maps can be downloaded for free from Sustrans (www.sustrans.org.uk) and the London Cycle Network (www.londoncyclenetwork.org.uk).
- Stop at red lights and avoid riding on pavements .

- Make eye contact with drivers at junctions.
- Use your arm to indicate when turning left or right.
- Be wary of parked cars' doors opening; give yourself about a metre's space.
- Don't cycle in the gutter.
- Use lights when appropriate.
- Wearing bright clothing can make you more visible.

Off-road safety code of conduct

- Only ride where you know it is legal to do so. Cyclists are not allowed to cycle on public footpaths (yellow waymarks). The only 'rights of way' open to cyclists are bridleways (blue markers) and unsurfaced tracks, known as byways, which are open to all traffic and waymarked in red.

- Canal tow paths: you need a permit to cycle on some stretches of tow path (www.waterscape.com). Remember that access paths can be steep and slippery, so always push your bike under low bridges and by locks.
- Always yield to walkers and horses, giving adequate warning of your approach.
- Don't expect to cycle at high speeds.
- Keep to the main trail to avoid any unnecessary erosion to the area beside the trail and to prevent skidding, especially in wet weather conditions.

Preparing your bicycle

Check the wheels, tyres, brakes and cables. Make sure you have a pump, a bell, and a set of lights.

Equipment

- A cycling helmet provides essential protection.
- Make sure you are visible by wearing light-coloured or bright clothing in daylight and sashes or reflective strips in failing light and darkness.
- Take extra clothes with you, depending on the season, and a wind/waterproof jacket.
- Carry a basic tool kit, a pump, a strong lock and a first aid kit.
- Always carry enough water.

Walk Map Legend

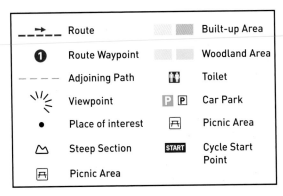

⇢	Route	Built-up Area	
➊	Route Waypoint	Woodland Area	
– – –	Adjoining Path	🚻	Toilet
☀	Viewpoint	P P	Car Park
●	Place of interest	⊞	Picnic Area
⌒	Steep Section	START	Cycle Start Point
⊞	Picnic Area		

Central

This area is home to Britain's political and royal power, with the twin draws of the Houses of Parliament and Buckingham Palace. It's also a magnet for shoppers who come for Covent Garden's stores, and art and history lovers who flock to the National Gallery, Tate Britain and the British Museum.

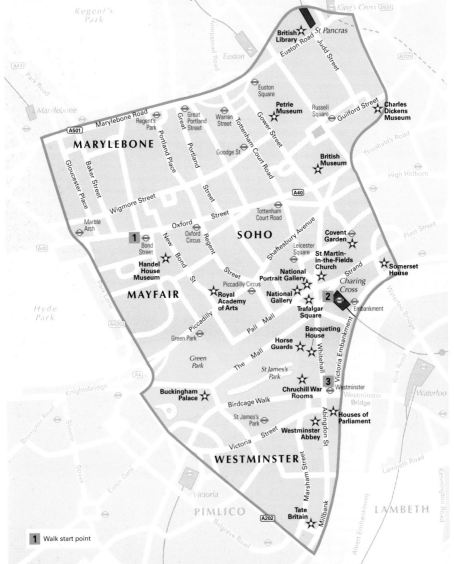

1 Walk start point

COVENT GARDEN MARKET

SELFRIDGES

THE QUEEN'S GUARD AT BUCKINGHAM PALACE

Unmissable attractions

Ancient and modern, frivolous and thought-provoking: whatever your interests, the heart of the capital can satisfy them. Even today central London is a patchwork of distinct neighbourhoods. In bookish Bloomsbury the world-leading British Museum would take days to explore fully. Continue south and Covent Garden will entertain you with opera, street theatre and boutiques. There are more shops around glossy Bond Street. A short walk to St James's Park will take you to Buckingham Palace. Political intrigues take centre stage at the Houses of Parliament, but to revel in the grandest of the capital's art galleries hop on a bus to a revitalised Trafalgar Square.

1 The West End
The flagship shopping district in London, formed around Regent Street, New Bond Street and Oxford Street, is home to department stores such as Selfridges and John Lewis, glitzy boutiques and expensive restaurants. Explore smaller streets such as Carnaby Street and Savile Row.

2 Buckingham Palace
The Queen's residence when she is in London is also the venue for state occasions, formal banquets and garden parties. The Palace is one of London's most photographed sights.

3 Houses of Parliament
The two Houses of Parliament, the Commons and the Lords, as well as innumerable offices are all covered by the title Palace of Westminster. Big Ben, atop London's famous landmark, is in fact the bell that strikes the hour.

4 British Museum
The Reading Room may request quiet, but the rest of the museum is a hive of activity with thousands of visitors a day discovering the treasures inside.

5 Covent Garden
While the Piazza is crammed with visitors and street entertainers, colourful side streets offer cafés and restaurants with terraces and shops.

BANQUETING HOUSE

MAP REF TQ301801

Easily overlooked by sightseers hurrying from the Houses of Parliament to Horse Guards Parade, the Banqueting House is all that remains of Whitehall Palace, which burned down in 1698. Inside, Inigo Jones' neo-classical design of 1622 introduced the 17th-century public to Palladian architecture. The ceiling of the magnificent main hall was painted by Rubens and celebrates James I's reign. As the monarch's favourite architect, Inigo Jones had enormous influence on how London looks even to this day. He designed the first public square (Covent Garden Piazza) and was involved in restoring St Paul's Cathedral.

BRITISH LIBRARY

MAP REF TQ300829

The British Library's new home was completed in 1997 and while the block-like, red-brick exterior (by architect Colin St John Wilson) dismayed some observers, there's no doubting the value of the treasures within. Among them are documents and books that have defined Britain: the Lindisfarne Gospels, the Magna Carta and Shakespeare's First Folio. Editions of global significance include Sultan Baybars' Qur'an, the Gutenberg Bible and the Indian legend the *Ramayana*. What's more, the British Library is open seven days a week and entry to the galleries is free. The range of exhibits is also surprising: although the library gets a copy of every new book published in the United Kingdom, you might not expect to see so many ancient maps on display or the detailed stamp collection. Musicians can read original music scores written by Bach, Mozart, Beethoven and Handel – and song lyrics by The Beatles. Or you can return to your childhood with the original version of *Alice's Adventures in Wonderland* by Lewis Carroll and first editions of Rudyard Kipling's *Jungle Book*. Special exhibitions are regularly scheduled and writers often give talks.

BRITISH MUSEUM

MAP REF TQ301817

The British Museum is arguably the finest museum of its kind in the world. It has unparalleled collections of art and antiquities that together document human civilisation across a number of cultures. There is far too much to see in one day; the best idea is to choose just a handful of galleries at a time. Most visitors head first for the museum's highlights, which include several Egyptian mummies, kept in a dimly lit room that adds to the eerie atmosphere. Also from Egypt is the Rosetta Stone, a slab of black basalt with text in three different languages that enabled experts to translate Egyptian hieroglyphics. As you might expect, ancient British history is especially well served by the museum. Must-see exhibits include the Mildenhall Treasure, Roman silverware unearthed in a Suffolk field; the Sutton Hoo Anglo-Saxon burial ship, also found in Suffolk; and Lindow Man, the prehistoric corpse of a man preserved in a peat bog.

Visiting the museum is not a dry experience and the curators try hard to interest children. A series of six family

and let thy feet
millenniums hence
be set in midst of knowledge

trails introduces youngsters to British history, ancient Greece and Egypt, and fantastical creatures. And during the school holidays there are activities, workshops and storytelling sessions.

One attraction at the British Museum that would be impossible to overlook is architect Norman Foster's Great Court, an airy, uplifting central courtyard.

BUCKINGHAM PALACE
MAP REF TQ290797

Although Buckingham Palace is not the most aesthetically pleasing of the royal properties – it's the result of a botched job by architects Edward Blore and John Nash, who began the conversion of the original 1703 house into a royal palace in 1825 – it remains at the heart of London. Today, it is not only the royal family who can enjoy the palace, because during August and September the State Rooms and gardens are opened to the public. It is fascinating to see not only the extravagant interiors but also how the rooms are organised. The Green Drawing Room is where guests gather before they are presented to the Queen, while banquets are held in either the State Dining Room or the vast Ballroom. With limited opening times, it is best to book a ticket in advance. However, the Queen's Gallery – the royal collection of art and treasures – off to the south side of the Palace, on Buckingham Gate, is open all year. On display are old masters as well as opulent exhibits such as jewellery, Fabergé eggs and Sèvres porcelain. Many of these exhibits were received by the royal family as gifts from foreign dignitaries over the past 500 years.

CHARLES DICKENS MUSEUM MAP REF TQ308822

From 1837 to 1839, Charles Dickens lived in this stern-looking four-storey Georgian house on the border of Bloomsbury and Clerkenwell. It was here that he completed *The Pickwick Papers*, his first full-length novel, and where he wrote *Nicholas Nickleby* and *Oliver Twist*. His study is complete with desk, letters and papers, memorabilia and most of the original décor.

London, of course, is replete with Dickens connections and if you walk south from the museum and go past Chancery Lane station, you'll come to Lincoln's Inn, which is the setting for Dickens' masterpiece *Bleak House*.

CHURCHILL WAR ROOMS
MAP REF TQ299797

It was in this bunker under Whitehall that crucial phases of the Second World War were planned by Winston Churchill.

Mirroring Churchill's famously no-nonsense persona, the rooms are functional yet sparsely furnished. They remain much as they were in 1945, with a map room for plotting troop movements with coloured pins, the Transatlantic Telephone Room for conversations with the President of the United States and a bedroom where Churchill took naps. You can learn much more about the man himself, including the brand of cigar he smoked and the hats he preferred, in the Churchill Museum. The interactive Lifeline display allows you to discover what happened on some of the most important dates in his life.

COVENT GARDEN

MAP REF TQ303809

London's first formal square was designed by the architect Inigo Jones in the 1630s. Bordered on one side by St Paul's Church and by the Royal Opera House on the other, Covent Garden Piazza is no longer the quiet residential square that the 17th-century landowner John Russell intended. Instead, it is a tourist nexus, attracting thousands to the arcade marketplace and the street performers outside. The result is that the lifts at Covent Garden tube station can be very congested: instead arrive at Leicester Square and walk up Long Acre – the distance between Covent Garden and Leicester Square stations is the shortest in the underground network. The shops within the piazza are carefully selected – no chain stores here. There is still a daily market in the North Hall, with arts and crafts stalls on Tuesday through to Sunday. On Mondays antiques dealers set up their stalls. Jubilee Market, on the corner of Southampton Street, mainly sells cheap and cheerful souvenirs. The surrounding area has also attracted some more prestigious retailers: Floral Street, Henrietta Street and King Street are lined with boutiques, and Southampton Street has a number of stores selling equipment for outdoor activities. Back on the square, St Paul's Church, also by Inigo Jones, is known as the Actors' Church. Inside there are plaques dedicated to Charlie Chaplin and Vivien Leigh, among others. Art historians may be interested to know that woodcarver par excellence Grinling Gibbons was buried here in 1721.

 Visit

ST JAMES'S PARK

The smallest and most central of London's parks is also one of its most appealing. Flanked by the Mall and Horse Guards, St James's Park has no shortage of visitors passing through or relaxing on the grass, making it fine territory for people-watching. You can also spot unusual waterfowl on the lake. From the excellent Inn the Park, visitors can enjoy the views of Buckingham Palace and the grand old buildings of Whitehall. If you feel the need for more space for a game of Frisbee or cricket, simply head across into neighbouring Green Park.

Visit

THE ICA AND THE HORSE HOSPITAL

Balance the grand old galleries and museums of the capital with a blast of the new; contemporary art seeps into central London via the ICA (the Institute of Contemporary Arts, on the Mall between Trafalgar Square and Buckingham Palace, and the Horse Hospital in Bloomsbury, a multi-storey arcade of radical art, from animation and photography to performance and fashion. Even the venues are interesting: the ICA is a gorgeous Georgian building while the Horse Hospital is a one-time stable. What's inside is bound to spark debate or delight.

Visit

LONDON TRANSPORT MUSEUM

Now that London's traditional red double-decker bus is almost a museum piece, replaced by the less popular 'bendy bus', you can visit the London Transport Museum to remind yourself of London's transport icons. From Harry Beck's classic tube map to the Hackney carriage, there is enough in this newly renovated museum to interest more than trainspotters – or should that be bus-spotters?

Through Mayfair in the style of James Bond

Ian Fleming's first novel *Casino Royale* introduced us to 007 in 1953. In 2006 Bond emerged updated in the film of the same name, portrayed by Daniel Craig. This walk captures some of Bond's glamour. Many of Mayfair's shops supply the royal family, and the locality is full of superb hotels. Home could be Albany, a block of bachelors' apartments. From here 007 could visit South Audley Street, for the royal gunmaker Purdey's and the Spy Shop. For relaxation, he could try Elemis Day Spa. And he might just end up at Claridge's for a dry martini – a nice place to end your walk too.

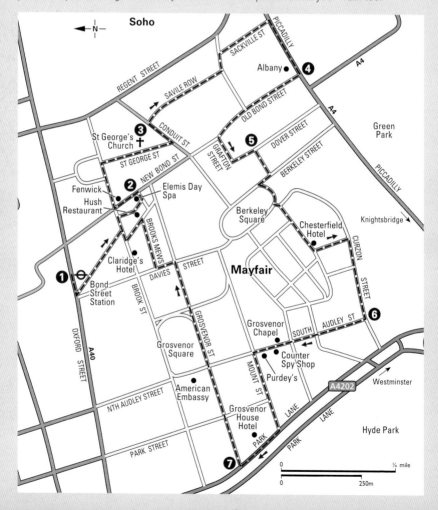

Route Directions

1 Turn left outside the tube station and sharp left into pedestrianised South Molton Street. At the end turn left into Brook Street. Cross the road and go along the cobbled right-hand alley, Lancashire Court, which opens into a courtyard. A few paces past Hush restaurant you'll find the Elemis Day Spa.

2 Turn left here and cross the road to reach the store, Fenwick. Turn right along Brook Street to reach Hanover Square. At the statue of the young William Pitt turn right into St George Street, past St George's Church and left at the end into Conduit Street.

3 Take the next right into the road of fine suits, Savile Row. At the end bear left and then right into Sackville Street. Turn right along Piccadilly and look out for the entrance to Albany's courtyard on your right.

4 Just past the auspicious-looking Burlington Arcade turn right into Old Bond Street and past several exclusive shops including those of Cartier, Mont Blanc and Tiffany. Turn left after Asprey into Grafton Street; which takes a 90-degree left bend, later becoming Dover Street.

5 Turn right along Hay Hill and then right again towards Berkeley Square, going over two crossings with the square on your right, to reach handsome Charles Street. Beyond the Chesterfield Hotel turn left along Queen Street and then right into Curzon Street.

6 Turn right into South Audley Street and its Counter Spy Shop, past the Grosvenor Chapel, then, at Purdey's (gunmakers), turn left into Mount Street. At the end turn right along Park Lane, past the Grosvenor House Hotel.

7 Turn right into Upper Grosvenor Street, past the American Embassy on Grosvenor Square, then turn left into Davies Street. Next, take the first right into Brooks Mews and go left along the narrow Avery Row. This brings you on to Brook Street. From here you can retrace your steps along South Molton Street, back to Bond Street tube from where the walk began.

Route facts

DISTANCE/TIME 2.75 miles (4.4km) 1h30

MAP AA Street by Street London

START/FINISH Bond Street tube station; grid ref TQ 285811

PATHS Paved streets

GETTING TO THE START Bond Street tube station is on the Central and Jubilee lines. This is in the congestion charge area and there are no parking facilities.

THE PUB The Audley, 41–43 Mount Street W1K 2RX Tel: 020 7499 1843

HANDEL HOUSE MUSEUM
MAP REF TQ288809

This museum, in exclusive Mayfair, is the site of a musical juxtaposition. It was the home of George Frideric Handel, the German-English composer, from 1723 to 1759. But in the late 1960s, the house next door, 23 Brook Street, was occupied by rock musician Jimi Hendrix – an odd coincidence that is acknowledged by the museum with a collection of photos of the guitar legend. But the real star here is the museum itself: as a recreation of the part of Handel's life spent in London it is remarkably detailed. The museum also offers a full programme of events, recitals, workshops and activities for young and old all year round.

HORSE GUARDS
MAP REF TQ300801

Horse Guards is famous for the straight-faced display by the Household Cavalry soldiers who are stationed outside every day. They are impassive in the face of the distraction techniques employed by sightseers. Look beyond the guards in their red tunics and you'll get a good view of the well-proportioned exterior by William Kent and John Vardy, who completed the building in 1751.

HOUSES OF PARLIAMENT
MAP REF TQ303795

British political power is concentrated in this majestic Gothic Revival building on the banks of the Thames. The Houses of Parliament, one of the world's earliest parliamentary democracies, are divided into the House of Lords and the House of Commons. The MPs of constituencies across Britain sit and deliberate in the Commons. Legislative proposals are then passed to the Lords for further consideration. During the summer recess, from early August to late September, British citizens can tour the House of Commons. The ticket office is adjacent to the Jewel Tower and is open from late July; tickets are also available online. Security is tight, so note what you can and cannot take inside. The 75-minute tour begins at the Norman Porch and enters the Queen's Robing Room, where she prepares for the annual State Opening of Parliament in November. From here, visitors pass through the Royal Gallery, the Prince's Chamber, the House of Lords Chamber and into the central Lobby, where MPs congregate for TV interviews. The tour concludes in St Stephen's Hall and the 11th-century Westminster Hall. The medieval Westminster Hall and the Jewel Tower are the only parts of the original Palace of Westminster that survived the fire of 1834. The Jewel Tower, or King's Privy Wardrobe, was built in 1365 to house Edward III's treasures. It is managed by English Heritage and you can visit all year round.

NATIONAL GALLERY
MAP REF TQ299806

You would need to set aside several days, or weeks even, to do justice to the National Gallery's collection of art. Instead of trying to see everything and exhausting yourself, home in on what interests you. There's plenty to choose from, with Italian Renaissance art in the

Sainsbury Wing a particular strength: there are works by Botticelli, Leonardo and Raphael. Recent acquisitions include Titian's sumptuous *Diana and Actaeon*, purchased jointly with the National Gallery of Scotland for £50m in 2008. Dutch masters, such as Vermeer and Van Dyck, occupy the North Wing, while the French Impressionists, including Monet, are a big draw for the East Wing. Reynolds, Constable, Turner and Gainsborough are just some of the home-grown artists on show, but as well as drinking in the art, also keep an eye on your surroundings: the building itself is of immense importance, a fact that is confirmed by its Grade I status. The National Gallery, as befits the country's leading art gallery, also has events, talks, film seasons and performances. Every month there is a full and changing programme of workshops, brunches and evening lectures.

NATIONAL PORTRAIT GALLERY MAP REF TQ300806

The National Portrait Gallery owns the world's largest collection of portraits. This surprisingly small space holds a collection of incredible quality and depth, making it a fascinating place for anyone interested in people, art or society. Royalty is represented by the portraits of the royal family in Room 33 and there are paintings of powerbrokers from Elizabethan, Stuart and Victorian times in subsequent rooms. These portraits tell the story of art, science, industry and politics through the ages, with the most contemporary characters appearing in the ground-floor galleries. Famous faces

here range from modern icon David Beckham (in a video by Sam Taylor-Wood) to one of the most recent additions, a portrait of J K Rowling, author of the Harry Potter novels. Like the National Gallery, there are frequent talks, films and events at the National Portrait Gallery, which celebrated its 150th year in 2006; visit the gallery's website for more details.

PETRIE MUSEUM
MAP REF TQ297821

Like some of archaeology's most elusive relics, the Petrie Museum of Egyptian Archaeology is rather hard to find. It is most easily reached from the back entrance of the British Museum: you walk past Waterstones, cross the road and the Petrie Museum will be seen advertised by a banner at the D M S Watson Science Library (part of the University College), where it occupies the first floor. Inside, expect a melange of antiquities retrieved by archaeologists from Egypt and Sudan, stored in

■ Activity

OUTDOOR ICE RINK

Don't forget your ice skates! In the depths of winter, when everyone needs cheering up, Somerset House hosts some of the most popular nights out in the capital with its open-air ice rink. The courtyard is frozen over and skaters of all abilities take to the ice. The ice rink is in operation from late November to late January and you need to book tickets in advance. It's not London's only open-air ice rink: there are also skating rinks at Hampton Court, the Tower of London, Kew Gardens and even the Natural History Museum.

old-fashioned wooden display cases. There are some interesting mysteries behind many of the fragments on display, some of which are unravelled in the summer storytelling season.

ROYAL ACADEMY OF ARTS
MAP REF TQ292806

Set back well away from the hurly-burly of Piccadilly, the Royal Academy was Britain's first formal art school. In early days it numbered John Constable and J M W Turner among its students. Its permanent collection, mostly hung in the John Madejski Fine Rooms, includes work by several eminent British artists, but the Academy is most famous for its major exhibitions, and especially the annual Summer Exhibition. This is an opportunity for amateur artists to shine because exhibits are decided by open audition – only 10 per cent of the works submitted make the final cut.

Architect Norman Foster redesigned the Sackler Wing, built from 1989 to 1991, adding an elegant glass elevator and flight of steps between the original 1666 house and the later Victorian galleries. It's a successful interaction of the traditional with the modern, leading to the new galleries above Burlington House. Whatever you do, don't miss Michelangelo's Taddei Tondo in the atrium.

ST MARTIN-IN-THE-FIELDS CHURCH MAP REF TQ806301

This church, on the northeastern corner of Trafalgar Square and distinguished by a grand portico, has a royal connection: it is the parish church for Buckingham Palace (the royal box is to the left of the gallery). It's also the focal point for a vibrant community that attends services and classical concerts. The concerts are staged at lunchtimes and sometimes in the evenings. Its basement Café in the Crypt is a good place for an inexpensive lunch, and families can take the children into the only brass-rubbing workshop in London next door; there are 90 brasses to choose from and staff are on hand to show how it is done.

SOMERSET HOUSE
MAP REF TQ307807

Somerset House is the collective name for three art galleries housed in this 18th-century riverside mansion: the Courtauld Gallery, the Gilbert Collection and the Hermitage Rooms. The house was built on the site of the Duke of Somerset's Tudor Palace and changed hands between various government departments and institutions several times during the 20th century. It has certainly embraced its current role with enthusiasm. Although the galleries are rather rarefied, Somerset House is also a versatile venue for live music (rock concerts rather than classical recitals) and even ice skating in the winter. The Courtauld contains art and sculpture from the early Italian Renaissance to 20th-century British pieces. The Gilbert Collection was donated to Somerset House five years before the death of collector Sir Arthur Gilbert in 2001. It is notable for focusing mainly on mosaics and includes some stunning pieces of *pietre dure* inlay work, but there are also vases, urns, plates and candelabra. The Hermitage has changing exhibits from the Winter Palace in St Petersburg.

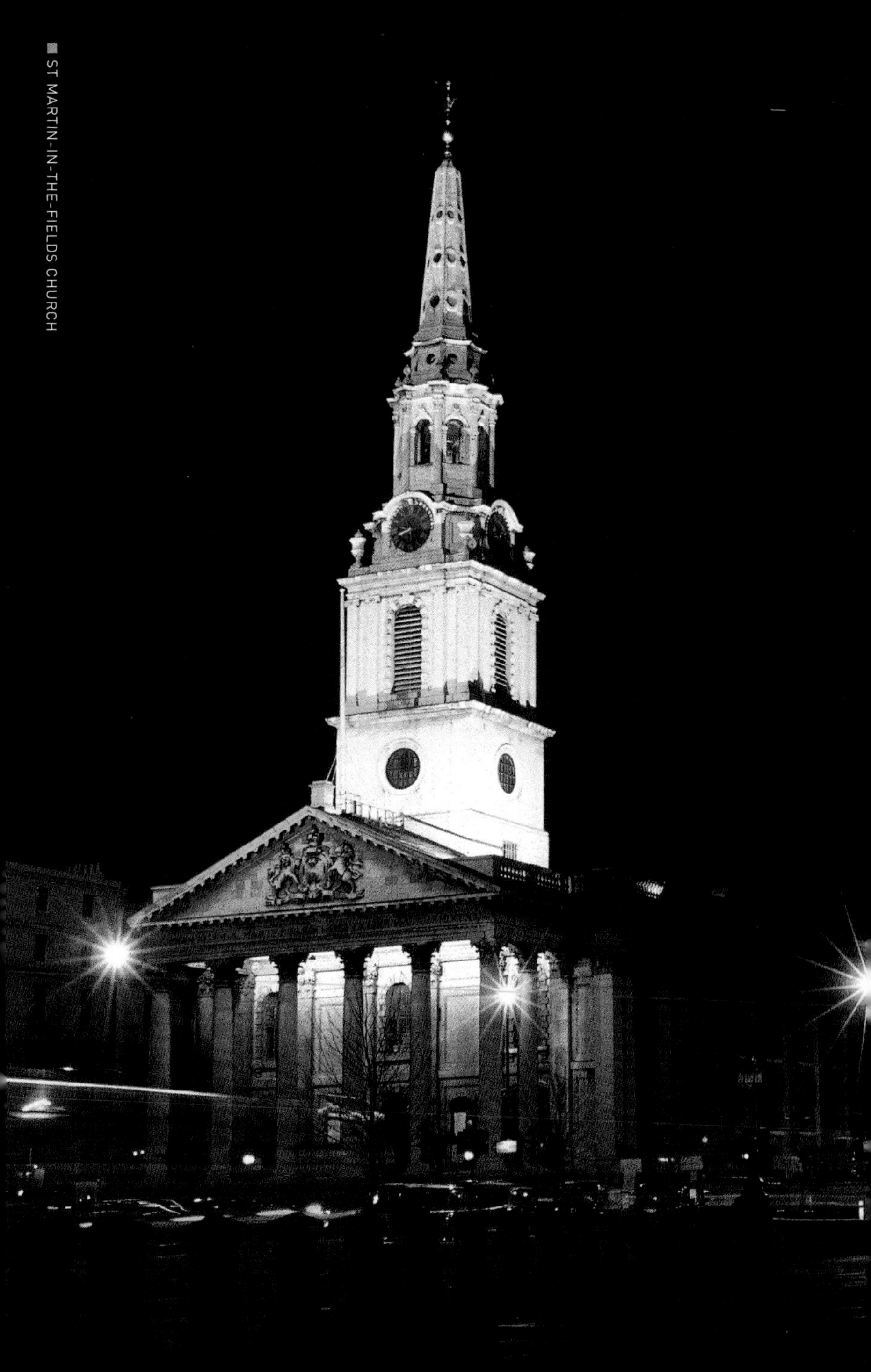

ST MARTIN-IN-THE-FIELDS CHURCH

From Charing Cross to Kensington Gardens

St James's Park was originally a swamp, but Henry VIII transformed it into a deer park. Charles II made it look as much like Versailles as possible, with avenues of trees and lawns, and opened the park to the public. Around 150 years later architect John Nash replaced the French layout with the English one you will see today, turning the canal into a lake and making over the park in a more romantic style.

Route Directions

1 From Charing Cross Station turn left into the Strand and left again into Northumberland Street. Bear left along Northumberland Avenue and, after a few paces, cross and turn right into Great Scotland Yard by Nigeria House.

2 At the end turn left into Whitehall, cross to the other side and head for the arch of Horse Guards Parade, where the guards are on duty for an hour at a time. Continue through the arch to a gravel square used for the Beating the Retreat ceremony in June.

3 Enter St James's Park to the left of the Guards Monument and follow the path that bears left around the lake, taking the first right-hand fork. Continue along this path, past weeping willow trees, to a blue bridge.

4 Cross the bridge, stopping half-way across to enjoy the views: westwards is Buckingham Palace and eastwards is Horse Guards Parade, where the skyline looks almost fairytale-like. Turn left, past the Nash Shrubberies, and leave the park on the right. Cross The Mall and enter Green Park from Constitution Hill.

5 Take the second path on the left and continue over another set of paths. At the next junction take the second path on the left. Where the next paths cross, take the left-hand path that inclines slightly to Hyde Park Corner.

6 Use the pedestrian crossing to first reach the central island and Wellington Arch, and then Hyde Park itself. Cross the road, Rotten Row, and follow the left-hand path through a rose garden with a cherub fountain. Dogs are not allowed in the Rose Garden, follow the dotted route on the map if necessary. After 350yds (320m) follow a path to the right of the Dell Restaurant and continue beside the Serpentine.

7 Walk under the Serpentine Bridge and up some steps on the right. Cross the bridge and enter Kensington Gardens. Take the middle path and continue ahead, ignoring other paths to eventually pass a bandstand, then turn right at the next opportunity.

8 At a junction bear left along the path that runs to the left of the gates to the Kensington Palace State Apartments. At the end turn left to reach Kensington Road. Pass the Royal Garden Hotel, Kensington Church Street and cross Kensington High Street to the tube station on the left.

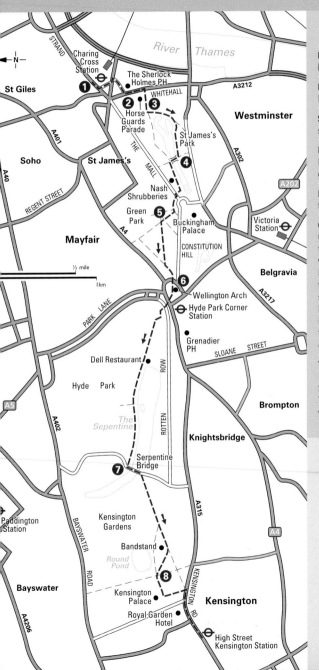

Route facts

DISTANCE/TIME 4.25 miles (6.8km) 2h30

MAP AA Street by Street London

START Charing Cross tube station; grid ref TQ 303803

FINISH High Street Kensington tube station; grid ref TQ 256796

PATHS Mainly tarmac paths through the parks

GETTING TO THE START Charing Cross railway and tube stations can be reached via the Northern and Bakerloo lines and from mainline stations in southeast London and beyond. There's a car park in St Martin's Lane, although this is in the congestion charging zone.

THE PUB The Grenadier, 18 Wilton Row, Belgrave Square SW1X 7NR Tel: 020 7235 3074; www.thespiritgroup.com

TATE BRITAIN MAP REF TQ301786

With the arrival of its sister gallery Tate Modern, Tate Britain has had much more exhibition space for its collection of 3,500 paintings. But even though it can now focus on British art from 1500 to the present day, the Victorian gallery still shows only a fraction of its vast collection. Rooms 1–17 are dedicated to British art from 1500 to 1900 – think sporting scenes by Stubbs, Turner's moody landscapes and illustrations by Blake. Turner also appears in several rooms in the Clore Galleries, added in 1987. Rooms 17–27 cover British art from 1900 to the present, with one room featuring work by Lucian Freud, Francis Bacon and Reg Butler, and another covering 1960s Pop Art. Talks by art experts and short courses can shed light on particular artists or periods. Whatever your taste, you should find something to entertain you at Tate Britain; if not, take the Tate boat down the Thames to the newer Tate Modern.

TRAFALGAR SQUARE

MAP REF TQ300804

Trafalgar Square is a monument to the British Empire. Named after the 1805 Battle of Trafalgar in the Napoleonic Wars, it honours Lord Horatio Nelson, the admiral who defeated the French at sea. A statue of Nelson, hand on heart, stands on top of a 185-foot (56m) column in the centre of the square, while two other statues in the square honour martial heroes of the period: Sir Henry Havelock and Sir Charles Napier. A third statue is of George IV, while, in artistic terms, the 1633 statue of Charles I by

Hubert Le Sueur remains one of the city's most significant statues. And there is the small matter of the fourth plinth, which until recently had remained empty since the square was commissioned in the 1820s. Architect John Nash completed the design in 1841, by which time funds were running low. This fourth plinth is now occupied by a series of modern artworks, including Marc Quinn's *Alison Lapper Pregnant*.

WESTMINSTER ABBEY

MAP REF TQ301794

The setting for many a royal story, Westminster Abbey dates from 1066, when Edward the Confessor was the first of many monarchs to be buried here. Under the Normans the abbey and its abbot became wealthy and powerful forces. During the Dissolution of the Monasteries in the 16th century its royal connections spared it the fate of other abbeys. It was Elizabeth I who returned Westminster Abbey to royal control in 1579; her effigy is in the Lady Chapel. The abbey has hosted all but two royal coronations. The monarch-to-be sits on St Edward's Chair during the ceremony. Burial here is an honour accorded not just to royalty and it is interesting to see the range of people commemorated here. They include eminent scientists (Darwin, Newton), actors, politicians and composers. Poets and writers occupy the south transept (Poets' Corner) and include Chaucer, Dickens and Kipling. The busts of the 17th-century poets Dryden, Jonson and Milton are worth seeking out. There are lectures, recitals and concerts throughout the year.

Westminster to Smithfield

The walk begins at Westminster Abbey then goes up Whitehall to the Strand, which was once one of the most influential thoroughfares in Britain, with many fine mansions, including Somerset House. Street names from here on give a clue as to the past inhabitants. Think of dukes and earls – Arundel, Surrey and Essex – as the Strand enters Aldwych (derived from 'Old Wic' meaning old settlement). The walk ends near the church of St Bartholomew-the-Great, which dates from 1123.

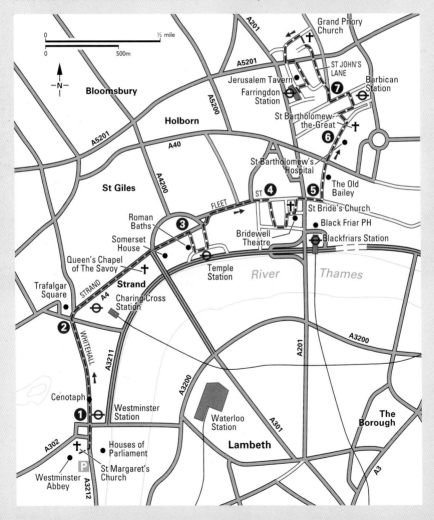

Route Directions

1 Leave Westminster tube following signs to the Houses of Parliament. Cross St Margaret Street to Westminster Abbey and the adjacent St Margaret's Church. Turn back along St Margaret Street and continue ahead as the road becomes Parliament Street, and then Whitehall. Follow it past the Cenotaph, a simple memorial to those people who died in both world wars, all the way to Trafalgar Square.

2 Turn right here and cross Northumberland Avenue. Turn right into the Strand, which links Westminster with the City of London. Turn right at Savoy Street, to see the Queen's Chapel of the Savoy; or carry on along the Strand, past Somerset House.

3 Turn right into Surrey Street, past the Roman Baths, left into Temple Place and left again along Arundel Street. The two churches in the middle of the road are St Mary-le-Strand and St Clement Danes. After these the road becomes Fleet Street.

4 After the banks of Lloyds and Child & Co turn right into Whitefriars Street. At the end turn left and left again into Dorset Rise. Take the next right into Dorset Buildings, past the Bridewell Theatre and along Bride Lane to St Bride's Church. Cross New Bridge Street.

5 You are now in Ludgate Hill. Turn left into the street called Old Bailey and continue to the Central Criminal Court, known as 'The Old Bailey' – it lies on the site of the notorious former Newgate Prison. Cross Newgate Street and follow Giltspur Street to reach St Bartholomew's Hospital.

6 Walk under the archway to the hospital, with the only remaining sculpture of King Henry VIII, to visit St Bartholomew-the-Less, the parish church of the hospital where Stuart architect Inigo Jones was baptised. Otherwise continue past the central square opposite Smithfield Market, and notice the marks on the stone wall left by a Zeppelin raid during the First World War. At St Bartholomew-the-Great turn left on West Smithfield, right on Long Lane and left into Hayne Street, then turn left again into Charterhouse Street.

Route facts

DISTANCE/TIME 4 miles (6.4km) 2h30

MAP AA Street by Street London

START Westminster tube station; grid ref: TQ 302797

FINISH Farringdon tube station; grid ref: TQ 316818

PATHS Paved streets

GETTING TO THE START Westminster tube station is on the Circle, District and Jubilee lines. This is in the congestion charge area and there are no parking facilities.

THE PUB The Bishop's Finger, 9 West Smithfield EC1A 9JR Tel: 020 7248 2341

7 At St John Street turn right and then bear left into St John's Lane. A few paces on is St John's Gate. Keep going and cross Clerkenwell Road to reach Grand Priory Church, bear left ahead to Jerusalem Passage, then turn left at the end, on to Aylesbury Street. Cross Clerkenwell Road and walk along Britton Street, turning right into Benjamin Street and left at the end to reach Farringdon tube where the walk ends.

■ PLACES OF INTEREST

Banqueting House
Whitehall SW1A 2ER
Tel: 0844 482 7777;
www.hrp.org.uk
Tube: Charing Cross,
Westminster.

British Library
96 Euston Road NW1 2DB
Tel: 0843 208 1144;
www.bl.uk
Tube: King's Cross.

British Museum
Great Russell Street
WC1B 3DG
Tel: 020 7323 8000;
www.britishmuseum.org
Tube: Russell Square,
Tottenham Court Road.

Buckingham Palace (and Queen's Gallery)
Buckingham Gate SW1A 1AA
Tel: 020 7766 7301;
www.royalcollection.org.uk
Tube: Green Park, Victoria.

Churchill War Rooms
King Charles Street
SW1A 2AQ
Tel: 020 7930 6961;
www.iwm.org.uk
Tube: Westminster.

Charles Dickens Museum
48 Doughty Street WC1N 2LX
Tel: 020 7405 2127;
www.dickensmuseum.com
Tube: Chancery Lane,
Russell Square.

Covent Garden
Tube: Covent Garden.

Handel House Museum
25 Brook Street W1K 4HB
Tel: 020 7495 1685;
www.handelhouse.org
Tube: Bond Street.

Horse Guards
Whitehall SW1A 2ER
Tube: Embankment,
Westminster.

The Horse Hospital
Colonnade, Bloomsbury
WC1N 1JD
Tel: 020 7833 3644;
www.thehorsehospital.com
Tube: Russell Square

Houses of Parliament
Parliament Square
SW1A 0AA
Tel: 0844 847 1672;
www.parliament.uk
Tube: Westminster.

Institute of Contemporary Arts
The Mall SW1Y 5AH
Tel: 020 7930 3647;
www.ica.org.uk
Tube: Charing Cross

Jewel Tower
Abingdon Street, Westminster
SW1 3JX
Tel: 020 7222 2219;
www.english-heritage.org.uk
Tube: Westminster.

London Transport Museum
Covent Garden WC2E 7BB
Tel: 020 7379 6344;
www.ltmuseum.co.uk
Tube: Covent Garden.

National Gallery
Trafalgar Square WC2N 5DN
Tel: 020 7747 2885;
www.nationalgallery.org.uk
Tube: Charing Cross.

National Portrait Gallery
2 St Martin's Place
WC2H 0HE
Tel: 020 7306 0055;
www.npg.org.uk
Tube: Charing Cross,
Leicester Square.

Petrie Museum
University College London,
Malet Place WC1E 6BE
Tel: 020 7679 2884;
www.petrie.ucl.ac.uk
Tube: Euston Square,
Goodge Street.

Royal Academy of Arts
Burlington House,
Piccadilly W1J 0BD
Tel: 020 7300 8000;
www.royalacademy.org.uk
Tube: Green Park,
Piccadilly Circus.

St Martin-in-the-Fields Church
Trafalgar Square WC2N 4JJ
Tel: 020 7766 1100; www.stmartin-in-the-fields.org
Tube: Charing Cross,
Leicester Square.

Somerset House
The Strand WC2R 0RN
Tel: 020 7845 4600;
www.somersethouse.org.uk
Tube: Holborn.

Tate Britain
Millbank SW1P 4RG
Tel: 020 7887 8888;
www.tate.org.uk
Tube: Pimlico.

Trafalgar Square
Tube: Charing Cross,
Leicester Square

Westminster Abbey
Parliament Square
SW1P 3PA
Tel: 020 7222 5152;
www.westminster-abbey.org
Tube: St James Park,
Westminster.

■ SHOPPING

Browns
23–27 South Molton Street
W1K 5RD. Tel: 020 7514 0016;
www.brownsfashion.com
Tube: Bond Street.
Stylish designer clothes.

Daunt Books
83 Marylebone High Street
W1U 4QW
Tel: 020 7224 2295;
www.dauntbooks.co.uk
Tube: Baker Street
Beautiful Edwardian
bookshop specialising in
travel.

Fortnum and Mason
181 Piccadilly W1A 1ER
Tel: 020 7734 8040;
www.fortnumandmason.co.uk
Tube: Piccadilly Circus.
Best known for its food hall,
the store also sells perfumes
and accessories.

Rococo Chocolates
45 Marylebone High Street
W1U 5HG. Tel: 020 7935 7780;
www.rococochocolates.com
Tube: Baker Street
Scrumptions handmade
chocolates

The Sanctuary
12 Floral Street WC2E 9DH

Tel: 01442 430330;
www.thesanctuary.co.uk
Tube: Covent Garden.
Oils, lotions, scrubs and
treatments at this spa.

Selfridges
400 Oxford Street W1A 1AB
Tel: 0800 123 400;
www.selfridges.com
Tube: Bond Street.
Selfridges is a central
alternative to Harvey Nichols.

Turnbull & Asser
71–72 Jermyn Street
SW1Y 6PF. Tel: 020 7808 3000;
www.turnbullandasser.com
Tube: Green Park,
Piccadilly Circus.
Fine shirts, worn by James
Bond and Prince Charles.

■ PERFORMING ARTS

Adelphi Theatre
Strand WC2R 0NS.
Tel: 020 7344 0055;
www.adelphitheatre.co.uk
Tube: Charing Cross.
Blockbuster shows.

Aldwych Theatre
Aldwych WC2B 4DF
Tel: 020 7379 3367;
www.aldwychtheatre.com
Tube: Covent Garden.
Catch plays and musicals.

Donmar Warehouse
41 Earlham Street WC2H 9LX
Tel: 0844 871 7624;
www.donmarwarehouse.com
Tube: Covent Garden.
Small-scale theatre stages
avant garde productions.

Odeon Leicester Square
22–24 Leicester Square,
WC2H 7JY. Tel: 0871 224
4007; www.odeon.co.uk
Tube: Leicester Square.
Multiplex cinema often used
for film premieres.

Ronnie Scott's Jazz Club
47 Frith Street, W1D 4HT
Tel: 020 7439 0747;
www.ronniescotts.co.uk
Tube: Leicester Square,
Tottenham Court Road.
Jazz gigs that live up to the
club's reputation. Late shows
on Friday and Saturday.

Royal Opera House
Bow Street WC2E 9DD
Tel: 020 7304 4000;
www.roh.org
Tube: Covent Garden.
The main venue for opera
and ballet.

**St Martin-in-the-Fields
Church**
Trafalgar Square WC2N 4JJ
Tel: 020 7766 1100; www.
stmartin-in-the-fields.org
Tube: Charing Cross,
Leicester Square.
Free lunchtime (and some
evening) concerts focus on
baroque music.

Wigmore Hall
36 Wigmore Street, W1U 2BP
Tel: 020 7935 2141;
www.wigmore-hall.org.uk
Tube: Bond Street.
Amazing acoustics in an
attractive and intimate
classical music venue.

Bar Italia

22 Frith Street
W1V 5PS
Tel: 020 7437 4520;
www.baritaliasoho.co.uk
Tube: Tottenham Court Road
This retro Italian coffeehouse
is said to turn out the finest
espressos in the capital. The
building it is in secured a
lasting place in history when
John Logie Baird invented the
television upstairs.

Beatroot

92 Berwick Street
W1F 0QD
Tel: 020 7437 8591;
www.beatroot.org.uk
Tube: Oxford Circus,
Tottenham Court Road
Refuel with fresh vegetarian
and vegan snacks, shakes,
salads and cakes at this
small Soho shop.

Flat White

17 Berwick Street W1F 0PT
Tel: 020 7734 0370;
www.flat-white.co.uk
Tube: Oxford Circus,
Tottenham Court Road
Get a caffeine fix at this
independent coffee shop in
Soho. The Australian-founded
café, favoured by Soho's
creative community, pours
some of the best coffee in the
capital (alongside sister café
the Milk Bar on Bateman
Street in Soho).

French House

49 Dean Street W1D 5BG
Tel: 020 7437 2799
Tube: Leicester Square
French House, which was
a favourite venue of French
leader General de Gaulle
during the war, is a cosy
restaurant masquerading as
a drinking den. The food in
this long- time Soho fixture is
a bit hit-and-miss, but the
wine list makes up for any
major food faux pas.

Imli

167–169 Wardour Street
W1F 8WR. Tel: 020 7287 4243;
www.imli.co.uk
Tube: Tottenham Court Road
Less expensive than its
swanky sibling Tamarind,
brightly lit Imli serves a
similarly imaginative menu
of Indian food with a
difference. Gone are heavy
sauces, replaced by a series
of small, tapas-style dishes
with light, zesty flavours.
There are three tasting
menus, all of which are
good value.

Inn the Park

St James's Park SW1A 2BJ
Tel: 020 7451 9999;
www.innthepark.com
Tube: St James's Park
The unobtrusive Inn the Park
overlooks the lake and, with
its wooden design, blends
well into leafy St James's
Park. You can sit inside or,
on sunnier days, on the
terrace or under the trees.
You'll still have to pay quite
a bit for the privilege, but
it's worth it. Sandwiches,
snacks, quiche, salad and
pots of tea are typical fare.

La Fromagerie

2–4 Maxon Street W1U 4EW
Tel: 020 7935 0341;
www.lafromagerie.co.uk
Tube: Baker Street,
Bond Street
After seeing and smelling
some of the world's best
cheeses in this shop, sit down
for a tasty snack in the café
area. Try home-baked bread,
a salad or, of course, some
fabulous cheese. Special
cheese-related events take
place on some evenings –
check the website for
upcoming events.

The Lamb

94 Lamb's Conduit Street
WC1N 3LZ
Tel: 020 7405 0713;
www.youngs.co.uk
Tube: Russell Square
The low ceilings and tiled
walls lend this pub an air
of tradition, although the
flower-filled hanging baskets
outside make the exterior
considerably more cheerful
than it would have been in

Victorian days. The beers, on tap from Youngs, are served as they should be and include plenty of guest ales. Standard bar food is available daily.

Leon
35 Great Marlborough Street W1F 7JE. Tel: 020 7437 5280; www.leonrestaurants.co.uk
Tube: Oxford Circus
Founded by chef Allegra McEvedy, Leon is a restaurant chain with a difference: it's dedicated to providing wholesome, healthy food from fresh, seasonal ingredients. Hot dishes include falafel and grilled chicken with aioli but you can also take away sandwiches, wraps and soups. There are branches of Leon on Regent Street, in Spitalfields and on the Strand and Bankside.

Monmouth Coffee Company
27 Monmouth Street WC2H 9EU.
Tel: 020 7379 3516; www.monmouthcoffee.co.uk
Tube: Covent Garden, Leicester Square
The Seven Dials area of Covent Garden is packed with tantalising shops, one of which sells London's best coffee beans. At the back of the Monmouth Coffee Company's shop is a small

café area where you can sample some of the company's freshly ground roasts – from all over the world – with a pastry or, at breakfast, some slices of wholemeal bread with honey.

Orrery
55 Marylebone High Street W1U 5RB. Tel: 020 7616 8000; www.orrery.co.uk
Tube: Baker Street
The friendly corner-shop café and deli of this fine-dining institution is a great place to pick up a tasty snack, such as Orrery's tartine of duck breast, goat's cheese or ham. There's also a blackboard of good specials.

Pizza Express
10 Dean Street W1D 3RW
Tel: 020 7437 9595; www.pizzaexpress.co.uk
Tube: Tottenham Court Road
This is no ordinary branch of the upmarket pizza chain. It's right in the heart of media-friendly Soho and has a highly regarded jazz club downstairs, for which you will need to book ahead.

Veeraswamy
99 Regent Street W1B 4RS
Tel: 020 7734 1401
Tube: Piccadilly Circus
London's oldest Indian restaurant has had a recent

makeover. It is now a sleek, elegant dining space and the food is as exquisite and delicately spiced as ever.

Villandry
170 Great Portland Street W1W 5QB
Tel: 020 7631 3131; www.villandry.com
Tube: Great Portland Street
You walk through the delicatessen to reach the restaurant in this centre of epicurean excellence. You can also get lunches to take away from the charcuterie bar or buy sandwiches and salads. Breakfast is served in the bar. A jazz trio plays in the bar on Saturday nights.

Wahaca
66 Chandos Place WC2N 4HG
Tel: 020 7240 1883; www.wahaca.co.uk
Tube: Charing Cross, Covent Garden, Leicester Square
Wahaca's mission is to serve Mexican market food – burritos, tacos and taquitos – without neglecting the environment. So, according to founder Thomasina Miers, waste is recycled and the food is ethically sourced. For families, this is a bright and breezy place in the heart of Covent Garden. And it would be a mistake to leave without trying the chocolate churros.

LLOYDS BUILDING

North & City

Northeast London, together with the City – the capital's financial heart – is London's most richly textured area, where money, law, art and successive waves of immigrants meet. Holborn, the setting for Dickens's novels, has changed little over the years and is the location for two of the capital's quirkiest museums, the Hunterian and Sir John Soane's Museum. To the north, Clerkenwell offers a concentration of excellent restaurants and some funky art galleries. This area rewards exploration on foot, whether you're plunging into the melée of Brick Lane's stalls, ethnic stores and curry houses or following in the grisly footsteps of Jack the Ripper. In terms of 'classic' London sights, the Tower of London and Sir Christopher Wren's Baroque St Paul's Cathedral are both hard to beat. For shopaholics Spitalfields Market has everything from food to fashionable clothes.

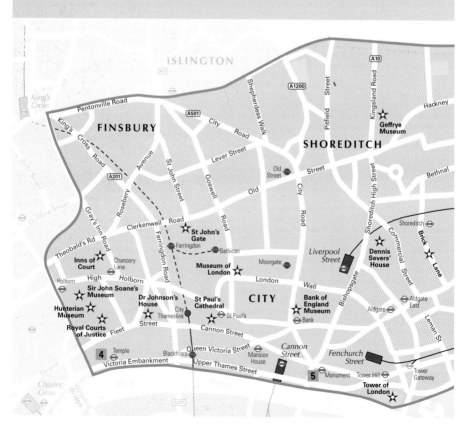

ST KATHARINE'S DOCK

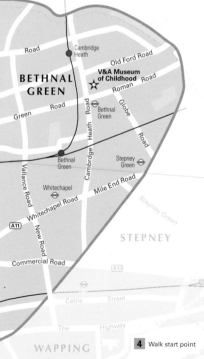

Road

Cambridge Heath

Old Ford Road

BETHNAL GREEN

V&A Museum of Childhood

Roman Road

Green Road

Bethnal Green

Globe Road

Cambrdge Heath Road

Bethnal Green

Stepney Green

Vallance Road

Whitechapel

Mile End Road

Stepney Green

Whitechapel Road

A11

New Road

STEPNEY

Commercial Road

A13

Cable Street

The Highway

WAPPING

4 Walk start point

CLERKENWELL

Unmissable attractions

In recent years the dynamic northeast of London has emerged as one of London's most intriguing corners. It was here that young artists set themselves up on inexpensive real estate, although the area is considerably pricier today. They paved the way for Clerkenwell's main attraction: a clutch of consistently exciting restaurants and a buzzing bar scene. Thank London's Asian community for Brick Lane, a street as vivacious by night as by day. But history hasn't been overwritten entirely: Charles Dickens would have recognised the Inns of Court, in the City, today. And 300-year-old St Paul's Cathedral still has the power to awe. As this is not London's museum district, Sir John Soane's Museum is still a well-kept secret.

4

5

1 **Brick Lane**
This vibrant street is home to a large Bangladeshi community, reflected in its street signs, its shops and its Balti restaurants.

2 **Shoreditch**
The colourful exterior of the Rivington Street Comedy Club. The street is a thriving area of restaurants, bars, cafés and entertainment venues.

3 **Tower of London**
First a palace, then a prison, the Tower is now one of the city's leading tourist venues and houses the Crown Jewels.

4 **Spitalfields**
The new Spitalfields Market development has a plethora of bars and restaurants.

5 **St Paul's Cathedral**
Sir Christopher Wren's masterpiece rises above the office workers and visitors strolling across the Millennium Bridge.

BANK OF ENGLAND MUSEUM MAP REF TQ327812

You don't have to be a financial wizard to find the Bank of England's free museum interesting: it's as much about politics and society as about economics. Money, of course, is the heart of the matter and here you can find out how banknotes are designed and made, or try lifting a gold ingot. The Bank of England has existed since the 17th century and its collection of notes and coins is incomparable – for example, it includes a £1 million note. The exhibits also cover the founding and management of Britain's financial system. There is an extensive collection of paintings and cartoons, all relating to the bank's work. The Bank of England has been at its location since 1734 but the building dates from 1934. A kid's corner offers quizzes and activities, but this museum is better suited to adults.

BRICK LANE MAP REF TQ338823

Brick Lane is one of the most cosmopolitan streets in London, a pulsating mélange of market stalls, shops, bars and many of London's cheapest (but not, unfortunately, best) curry restaurants, which are mostly run by the area's Bangladeshi community. It takes its name from the brick and tile manufacturing workshops that sprang up in the Middle Ages; more recently it lent its name to Monica Ali's novel about everyday life in London's Asian communities. Brick Lane is best visited on either Sunday morning, for the street market, or in the evening, when it throngs with Londoners hopping from one nightspot to another.

Off to the side are some interesting courtyards, such as the Old Truman Brewery, now populated by young artists and designer boutiques. At 159 Brick Lane, the Beigel Bake has carved a niche in East End folklore with its satisfying bagels, sold 24 hours a day.

DENNIS SEVERS' HOUSE MAP REF TQ335820

When you open the front door of this 18th-century house you step back in time into the house of a family of Huguenot silk weavers. The unique attraction of this house, created by the late Dennis Severs, is that it is not a sterile collection of antiques but rather a sensory extravaganza spread across the whole house from cellar to bedrooms via the kitchen, eating parlour and smoking room. Severs not only collected all the items you could expect to find in houses from many different periods, he also introduced smells and sounds that serve to suggest that the occupants have only just left the rooms: floorboards creak, clocks chime and candles burn. Severs called the experience 'still-life drama'. Pay attention to the details and you'll get the most out of the experience.

■ Activity

JACK THE RIPPER WALK

Brick Lane was one of the haunts of 19th-century serial killer Jack the Ripper. This entertaining guided tour of the killer's East London hunting ground by Original London Walks is the most authoritative tour in the capital. It begins at Tower Hill tube station on certain evenings and concludes in the Ten Bells pub, where many victims – and perhaps the killer – drank.

DR JOHNSON'S HOUSE

MAP REF TQ313812

The City of London, the financial core of the capital, hasn't changed much in 200 years. This red-brick building remains the only 18th-century house open to the public in the City. From 1748 to 1759 it was the home of Dr Samuel Johnson, the journalist, poet and lexicographer, who compiled the first English dictionary here. The panelled rooms have been restored to period splendour with Queen Anne furniture, prints and portraits.

GEFFRYE MUSEUM

MAP REF TQ335832

Get some ideas for refreshing your home at this museum of English domestic interior decoration. Almost every fad, fashion and furnishing from 1600 to the present is displayed or described in rooms organised by period; you can walk from a thorough re-creation of a Georgian living room into a modern loft conversion living space. A new wing houses a café, while there are plenty of good and inexpensive eateries near by. The museum is set inside a series of converted 18th-century almshouses surrounded by period gardens.

HUNTERIAN MUSEUM

MAP REF TQ308813

The Hunterian Museum is one of the capital's more curious museums and is likely to arouse the interest of those with a taste for the unusual. As it is the museum of the Royal College of Surgeons, it is packed with exhibits relating to the college's work. There is a large gallery of surgical instruments

■ Visit

CHRIST CHURCH

Christ Church is one of London's most marvellous churches. It lies to the southeast of Spitalfields market and was designed by Nicholas Hawksmoor in the early 18th century as one of 50 new churches intended to serve an expanding London. However, only six of the churches were ever completed and the first of them, Christ Church, has been undergoing restoration since the 1970s. Built in Hawksmoor's trademark style of abrupt layers – a Tuscan porch is topped by a series of arches and then a spire – it is returning to its former glory. Fundraising events, including the Spitalfields Festival in December, are held at the church.

and medical equipment charting the development of surgery since the 18th century – when an anaesthetic was likely to be no more than a stiff drink. The Crystal Gallery has more than 3,000 specimens of human and animal skeletons collected by John Hunter, 18th-century anatomist and Surgeon General of the British Army. Exhibits include the preserved brain of 19th-century mathematician Charles Babbage. The redevelopment of the museum means that the collections are displayed in an environment as clean, bright and modern as an operating theatre. There is nothing particularly grisly here, although you should be prepared to see giants, mummified hands and jars containing preserved organs! There are regular lectures on science and natural history by experts from the Royal Institution and Sir John Soane's Museum.

The Inns of Court

The area between Temple and Fleet Street is home to some fine buildings that survived the Great Fire, and to walk through this august legal institution is to take a step back in time. Charles Dickens set some of his novels in the hidden alleys and squares here. When you reach Fountain Court you'll see how little it can have changed in 200 years. The place is most atmospheric at dusk, when the Victorian street lamps are lit. It is here that Tom meets his sister Ruth in *Martin Chuzzlewit*. The Middle Temple feels like a village. Dickens describes how young Tom felt about going to work in the Temple: '... he turned his face towards an atmosphere of unaccountable fascination, as surely as he turned it to the London smoke – until the time arrived for going home again and leaving it, like a motionless cloud behind'.

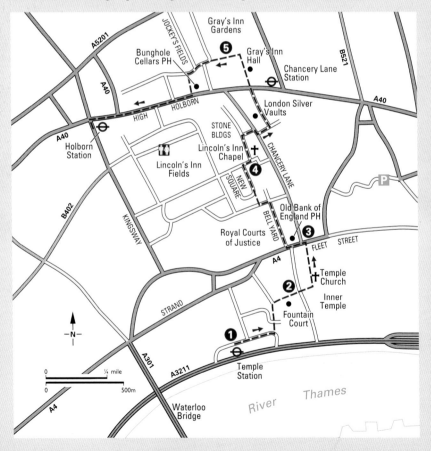

Route Directions

1 Turn left at the exit to Temple tube and up a set of steps. Turn right into Temple Place. At the end go left into Milford Lane and continue ahead up another series of steps, into Inner Temple. Turn right by The Edgar Wallace pub into Devreux Court, walk under the archway and bear right to go down the steps to Fountain Court.

2 Bear left to pass the Middle Temple Hall and go under an archway into Middle Temple, past a small fountain and garden and up the steps, then continue through some cloisters to reach the Temple Church, featured in *The Da Vinci Code* film. Carry on to the left of the church along a cobbled alley to pass under an archway and emerge on to Fleet Street.

3 Turn left along Fleet Street and cross at the pedestrian lights. After the Old Bank of England pub turn right into Bell Yard and continue ahead on the path that runs alongside the Royal Courts of Justice. Turn left and then right through the archway into New Square; follow the avenue of trees.

4 Take the path on the far right past Lincoln's Inn Chapel to reach Stone Buildings and, ahead, go through the gates that lead to Chancery Lane, via a narrow lane. Cross this road and turn left into the street called Southampton Buildings. After just 20yds (18m) this veers sharply left, past the London Silver Vaults. At the end cross High Holborn and pass through a gateway to Gray's Inn on the right. A few paces further, after Gray's Inn Hall, turn left into Field Court.

5 Continue to the end then turn right and go up the steps into Jockey's Fields. Bear left and take the second road on the left, Hand Court. Just past the Bunghole Cellars at the end, turn right along High Holborn to reach Holborn tube.

Route facts

DISTANCE/TIME 1.5 miles (2.4km) 1h30

MAP AA Street by Street London

START Temple tube station; grid ref TQ309808

FINISH Holborn tube station; grid ref TQ306815

PATHS Paved streets and alleyways

GETTING TO THE START
Temple tube station is on the Circle and District lines. This is in the congestion charge area and there are no parking facilities.

THE PUB The Cittie of Yorke, 22 High Holborn
WC1V 6BS
Tel: 020 7242 7670

INNS OF COURT & ROYAL COURTS OF JUSTICE

MAP REF TQ310812

London has four Inns of Court, where the capital's legal profession works. Taking a walk through Lincoln's Inn, Gray's Inn, Inner and Middle Temple is one of the best ways of getting a taste of Dickensian and even Shakespearean London – they are some of the least changed parts of the city. Lincoln's Inn was where the interminable case of Jarndyce and Jarndyce at the heart of Charles Dickens's *Bleak House* ground its way through the courts. Near by is Lincoln's Inn Fields, which was once a popular place for settling duels, but these days you're more likely to see a closely fought tennis match here.

Middle Temple is where William Shakespeare's *Twelfth Night* was premiered in 1602, under the wood-beamed roof. At Gray's Inn only the gardens, which were laid out in 1606 by philosopher Sir Francis Bacon, are open to the public. This is a quiet, beguiling place to walk through, but visit during the week because only one of the gates is open at the weekend.

The Royal Courts of Justice are where many of Britain's major civil cases are decided; the pinnacles and spires of the Gothic Revival building resemble a place of worship. Fleet Street, which passes along the south side of the Royal Courts of Justice, was once the stamping ground of the nation's newspaper reporters, but they have moved with their paper's offices to Canary Wharf and other less central sites. Further along Fleet Street, the Old Bailey (properly called the Central Criminal Court) is where many of the most serious criminal cases are heard. Members of the public are allowed to watch proceedings from the gallery but there are strict entrance regulations.

MUSEUM OF LONDON

MAP REF TQ322816

As one of the world's oldest capital cities, London has more than enough tales to tell. This modern museum, organised in chronological order, picks up London's story from its first chapter as a Roman settlement in AD 50 and narrates the city's progress through successive periods. The first section even describes the area pre-Londinium, with some absorbing tableaux: the River Wall displays some 300 items dredged from the Thames, including bronze and iron swords flung into the river to appease the gods. Mosaics and marble statues are the highlights of the Roman section, while a new Medieval Gallery skips through 1,000 years of history from the 5th to 16th centuries as London grew into one of the world's key ports.

After this period the Great Fire of London sparked a period of rebuilding and then boom time, as London became the commercial centre of the world. In the 18th century, London soaked up foreign influences in fashion, food and the arts. A highlight here is the opulent gold-leafed coach that is still used in the annual Lord Mayor's Show.

The museum opened five new galleries in 2010, the Galleries of Modern London, which relate the story of London from 1666 to the present day.

ST JOHN'S GATE

MAP REF TQ307814

Over the years, Clerkenwell has become one of the most upwardly mobile areas of London, with trendy eateries popular with the banking and media people who work locally. (The area's edgier, artier denizens have gradually moved east to Hoxton and Shoreditch.) Historically, however, Clerkenwell had strong monastic traditions and its most famous order was the Knights Hospitallers of St John of Jerusalem. The order was founded to provide both medical and monetary assistance to soldiers fighting in the medieval Crusades; a modern offshoot is the St John Ambulance Service. The only remaining portion of the knights' medieval priory is this Tudor gatehouse and the Norman church, surrounded by office buildings just off the Clerkenwell Road. Inside the gatehouse a museum tells the story of the Knights of St John and includes exhibits such as suits of armour, an altarpiece and illuminated manuscript.

Across the road, Clerkenwell Green is one of the most pleasant village greens remaining in the centre of the capital. It has a history of radicalism, being associated with Marx, Lenin and the Communist Party for some of the 20th century. Today, you're more likely to find gastropubs here rather than 'Reds'.

ST PAUL'S CATHEDRAL

MAP REF TQ317821

St Paul's dome, 354ft (108m) high – the only domed cathedral in Britain – rises unmistakably above the buildings of the north bank of the River Thames. The

◼ Insight

HATTON GARDEN

This road, running parallel to Farringdon Road, is the centre of London's jewellery and diamond-dealing businesses. It is mainly importers and wholesalers who are based here, so it is not the best place for shopping, although more and more retail outlets are opening. You can also see some of London's few remaining pawnbrokers, identified by three brass balls hanging from the door.

cathedral was commissioned after the Great Fire destroyed the original in 1666. Leading architect Sir Christopher Wren mixed classical and Gothic architecture in its design, although it is the sense of scale that impresses most visitors: the dome is second in size only to St Peter's in Rome; inside, the dome and galleries appear even larger. The interior is a mass of soaring arches, intricate carving and gilding. To the right of the nave, steps lead up to the Whispering Gallery; if you're here early enough and the cathedral is quiet you can hear a whisper from the opposite side of the nave, thanks to the acoustics.

Although it is a bit of a hike up the 530 steps to the dome's Golden Gallery, the climb is worth it for the views across London – they rival those from the London Eye, but are cheaper! The tombs of the Duke of Wellington, Admiral Nelson and Sir Christopher Wren are in the crypt, as is the cathedral's treasury, which was plundered in 1810 and now consists of gold and silver items loaned from other churches. The cathedral celebrates its 300th anniversary in 2008.

SIR JOHN SOANE'S MUSEUM MAP REF TQ307814

Often described as London's best-kept secret, this museum contains the fruit of decades of collecting by Sir John Soane, Professor of Architecture at the Royal Academy. He would open his house to visitors on the day before and the day after one of his lectures, and here they could see a crowded cornucopia of sculpture, paintings, carvings, furniture and curios spread across the floorspace of three town houses. Today the rooms are organised according to Soane's original design; he even planned the ideal route around his collection.

Highlights include the Picture Room, which has hinged screens to extend hanging space; three Canalettos take pride of place in the New Picture Room. Given the variety of his tastes, it isn't so surprising to come across the 3,000-year-old sarcophagus of Pharaoh Seti I in the museum's crypt; and several important Roman marbles and statues. Soane also built up an internationally acknowledged collection of Chinese tiles. Whether you're an art student or not, you will find something intriguing here. It is worth noting that due to the limited space inside and the museum's popularity, there may be queues on Saturdays, so try to get there early.

TOWER OF LONDON
MAP REF TQ336806

As firm a fixture on tourists' itineraries as Buckingham Palace, the Tower of London is equally as tied up with royal history. The Tower first came to national prominence in the 13th century, but the oldest building on the site dates from the 11th century. It was initially used as an armoury, fortress and royal residence and only later became a prison; the buildings around Tower Green include the Bloody Tower, where many of the most famous and important prisoners were kept. Traitors' Gate was the place where those accused of treason arrived by boat. Hourly tours led by Beefeaters are recommended if you have children – the scarlet-clad Beefeaters are experts at bringing the stories to life. The armouries exhibition in the White Tower is an enthralling series of weapons and armour, but the highlight of a visit for most people is seeing the Crown Jewels, on display in the Waterloo Barracks. Although you're herded through on a moving travelator, it's hard to miss the world's largest cut diamond, the Star of Africa, or the Imperial State Crown.

V&A MUSEUM OF CHILDHOOD MAP REF TQ351828

The Museum of Childhood underwent a major revamp in 2006, when the V&A, which manages the museum, added a new entrance and expanded the learning centre. The exhibits, which cover more than 400 years, will cause many a bout of reminiscence. There are model trains and board games, but the museum also holds Britain's largest collection of doll's houses with some examples dating from the 17th century and others with royal connections. The collection of teddy bears at the museum is sourced from all parts of the world. For children, there are storytelling activities during school holidays and at weekends.

The Route of the Great Fire of London

Londoners in the 17th century must have wondered what had hit them when, within months of fighting off the Great Plague, a fire of monumental proportions began at a bakery in Pudding Lane. It wasn't until 2am on 2 September 1666 that the baker discovered the fire, and within five days the city of half-timbered houses and pitch-covered buildings that Shakespeare had known had gone up in smoke. Although 13,000 houses, 87 churches and 40 livery halls were destroyed, incredibly, only eight people lost their lives, although many later perished after they were left homeless.

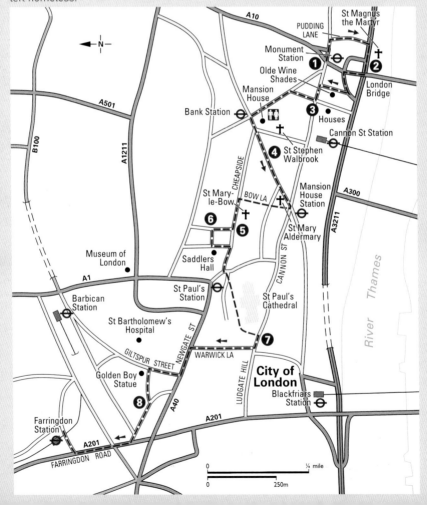

Route Directions

1 Take the Fish Street Hill exit from the tube station and bear right towards the Monument. Follow the cobbled street for 20yds (18m) to see the plaque that marks the spot on the corner of Pudding Lane where the ill-fated bakery once stood. Bear right, then cross Lower Thames Street at the pedestrian crossing to reach St Magnus the Martyr Church.

2 A few paces further to the right of the church, climb a set of steps and, ignoring the first exit, continue to arrive on the west side of London Bridge. Continue ahead, away from the river, along King William Street and shortly turn left along Arthur Street and then sharp right into Martin Lane, past the Olde Wine Shades. At the end turn left into Cannon Street. (For a detour to see the red-brick houses that survived the fire, turn next left into Laurence Poultney Hill.)

3 Cross the road and turn right into Abchurch Lane. At the end bear left along King William Street towards Bank tube station. Keep to the left, past the front of Mansion House, and notice the street on the left, Walbrook: this is the site of one of Wren's finest churches, St Stephen Walbrook Church. Turn left into Queen Victoria Street.

4 Continue ahead, then turn right into Bow Lane, past St Mary Aldermary and a row of shops, to St Mary-le-Bow at the end. Turn left into Cheapside which, despite being the widest road in the City, also went up in flames.

5 Cross this road, turn right into Wood Street. On your right was the site of one of London's debtors' prisons.

6 Turn left into Goldsmith Street and, at the Saddlers Hall opposite, turn left and rejoin Cheapside. Turn right and cross the pedestrian crossing to St Paul's Cathedral. Walk through the churchyard, bear left to reach Ludgate Hill.

7 Turn right and right again into Ava Maria Lane, which becomes Warwick Lane. At the end turn left along Newgate Street. At the traffic lights turn right along Giltspur Street, then left into Cock Lane.

8 Where another road meets it, turn right along Snow Hill, past an angular building, and right at Farringdon Street (which becomes Farringdon Road). At the second set of traffic lights turn right, to reach Farringdon tube, where the walk ends.

Route facts

DISTANCE/TIME 2.25 miles (3.6km) 2h

MAP AA Street by Street London

START Monument tube station; grid ref: TQ 328808

FINISH Farringdon tube station; grid ref: TQ 316818

PATHS Paved streets

GETTING TO THE START Monument tube station is on the District and Circle lines. This is in the congestion charge area and there are no parking facilities.

THE PUB Ye Olde Watling, 29 Watling Street EC4M 1BR Tel: 020 7653 9971

■ PLACES OF INTEREST

Bank of England Museum
28 Threadneedle Street
EC2R 8AH
Tel: 020 7601 5545;
www.bankofengland.co.uk
Tube: Bank.

Brick Lane
Tube: Aldgate East,
Liverpool Street.

Christ Church
Fournier Street, Spitalfields
E1 6QE
Tel: 020 7859 3035; www.
christchurchspitalfields.org
Tube: Aldgate East,
Liverpool Street.

Dennis Severs' House
18 Folgate Street E1 6BX
Tel: 020 7247 4013;
www.dennissevershouse.co.uk
Tube: Liverpool Street.

Dr Johnson's House
17 Gough Square EC4A 3DE
Tel: 020 7353 3745;
www.drjohnsonshouse.org
Tube: Blackfriars, Chancery
Lane, Temple.

Geffrye Museum
136 Kingsland Road E2 8EA
Tel: 020 7739 9893;
www.geffrye-museum.org.uk
Tube: Liverpool Street (then
bus).

Hatton Garden
Tube: Farringdon.

Hunterian Museum
Royal College of Surgeons,
35–43 Lincoln's Inn Fields
WC2A 3PE
Tel: 020 7869 6560;
www.rcseng.ac.uk/museums
Tube: Holborn.

Inns of Court
Tube: Chancery Lane,
Holborn.

Museum of London
150 London Wall EC2Y 5HN.
Tel: 020 7001 9844;
www.museumoflondon.org.uk
Tube: Barbican, St Paul's.

Royal Courts of Justice
Strand WC2 2LL
Tel: 020 7947 6000
Tube: Charing Cross,
Chancery Lane.

St John's Gate
St John's Lane EC1M 4DA
Tel: 020 7324 4000;
www.sja.org.uk
Tube: Farringdon.

St Paul's Cathedral
EC4M 8AD
Tel: 020 7246 8350;
www.stpauls.co.uk
Tube: St Paul's.

Sir John Soane's Museum
13 Lincoln's Inn Fields
WC2A 3BP
Tel: 020 7405 2107;
www.soane.org
Tube: Holborn.

Tower of London
EC3N 4AB
Tel: 0844 482 7777;
www.hrp.org.uk
Tube: Tower Hill.

V&A Museum of Childhood
Cambridge Heath Road
E2 9PA. Tel: 020 8983 5200;
www.vam.ac.uk/moc
Tube: Bethnal Green.

■ SHOPPING

Angela Flanders
96 Columbia Road E2 7QB
Tel: 020 7739 7555;
Tube: Old Street
Traditional perfumier in
beautiful Victorian shop;
only open Sun.

A Gold
42 Brushfield Street E1 6AG
Tel: 020 7247 2487
Tube: Liverpool Street.
The best sandwiches in
Spitalfields and traditional
British foods.

Antoni & Alison
43 Rosebery Avenue
EC1R 4SH
Tel: 020 7833 2141;
www.antoniandalison.co.uk
Tube: Farringdon.
Designer label clothes.

Columbia Road
Flower Market
Columbia Road E2 7RH
Tube: Liverpool Street, Old
Street, then bus or walk.
Flowers and plants at this
famous Sunday market.

Condor Cycles
51 Grays Inn Road
WC1X 8PP
Tel: 020 7269 6820;
www.condorcycles.com
Tube: Chancery Lane.
Historic shop with clothing,
accessories and bikes.

Labour & Wait
18 Cheshire Street E2 6EH
Tel: 020 7729 6253;
www.labourandwait.co.uk

Tube: Liverpool Street.
Chic range of home and
garden products.

Nicholas James
16–18 Hatton Garden
EC1N 8AT. Tel: 020 7242 8000;
www.nicholasjames.com
Tube: Farringdon.
One of a new breed of
jewellers.

Persephone Books
59 Lamb's Conduit Street
WC1N 3NB
Tel: 020 7242 9292;
www.persephonebooks.co.uk
Tube: Holborn, Russell
Square.
Reprints forgotten 20th-
century classics by mostly
women writers.

Prick Your Finger
260 Globe Road E2 0JD
Tel: 020 8981 2560
Tube: Bethnal Green
Haberdashery selling yarn,
plus craft classes.

Space EC1
25 Exmouth Market
EC1R 4QL
Tel: 020 7837 1344;
Tube: Farringdon.
Funky homeware and kitsch
gifts in a small shop.

Spitalfields Market
Commercial Street
E1 6AA.
www.visitspitalfields.com
Tube: Liverpool Street.
Mon–Wed shops only, Thu
antiques, Fri fashion, Sun
shops and stalls.

This Shop Rocks
131 Brick Lane E1 6SE
Tel: 020 7739 7667
Tube: Liverpool Street.
Vintage clothing in a district
full of secondhand shops

Verde & Co
4 Brushfield Street,
Spitalfield E1 6AG
Tel: 020 7247 1924
Tube: Liverpool Street.
Fresh pasta and charcuterie.

■ ACTIVITIES

Jack the Ripper Walk
Original London Walks
Tel: 020 7624 3978;
www.walks.com

**Museum of London
Walks and Tours**
150 London Wall EC2Y 5HN
Tel: 020 7001 98440;
www.museumoflondon.org.uk
Tube: Barbican, Moorgate,
St Paul's.Seasonal walks led
by expert guides.

National Trust Walks
2 Willow Road NW3 1TH
Tel: 020 7435 6166;
www.nationaltrust.org.uk
Monthly guided walks around
Spitalfields.

■ PERFORMING ARTS

The Barbican
Silk Street EC2Y 8DS
Tel: 020 7638 4141;
www.barbican.org.uk
Tube: Barbican.
Europe's largest
arts centre.

Hackney Empire
291 Mare Street E8 1EJ
Tel: 020 8510 4500;
www.hackneyempire.co.uk
Train: Hackney Central.
This extravagantly decorated
Edwardian theatre is the vital
venue for shows, concerts,
musicals and pantomimes
in the East End of London.

Sadler's Wells
Rosebery Avenue EC1R 4TN
Tel: 0844 412 4300;
www.sadlerswells.com
Tube: Angel.
London's top dance venue.

■ EVENTS

Baishakhi Mela
Brick Lane E1
www.baishakhimela.org.uk
The Bengali New Year
celebrations in mid-May
is Europe's largest Asian
festival, with live music
and aromatic food stalls.

Ceremony of the Keys
Tower of London, Tower Hill
EC3N 4AB
Tel: 020 3166 6278;
www.hrp.org.uk
Tube: Tower Hill.
Apply in writing to witness
the nightly ritual of locking
the gates.

London Art Fair
Business Design Centre,
52 Upper Street N1 0QH
www.londonartfair.co.uk
Tube: Angel.
Annual art fair, Jan.

The Ambassador

55 Exmouth Market
EC1R 4QE
Tel: 020 7837 0009; www.
theambassadorcafe.co.uk
Tube: Farringdon

This new café and restaurant in trendy Exmouth Market offers a sparse but stylish dining room, robust cooking and good wines. Mains can be pricey, given that they favour cheaper cuts (coley instead of cod, for example), but Tobias Jilsmark's cooking is worth the outlay.

Cittie of Yorke

22 High Holborn
WC1V 6BN
Tel: 020 7242 7670
Tube: Chancery Lane

Described by one journalist as a cathedral among pubs, this has a spectacular interior as befits a Grade II listed building. It gets busy at the end of the working day so drop in for a look during the day or later in the evening.

E Pellici

332 Bethnal Green Road
E2 0AG
Tel: 020 7739 4873
Tube: Bethnal Green

An unsung London landmark, Pellicci's family-owned café is a time capsule that has been serving fry-ups and expressos to east Londoners

since 1900. The art deco interior has been unchanged for decades (as has the good-natured chat) and offers respite from homogenous high street eateries.

Frizzante

Hackney City Farm,
1a Goldsmith's Row E2 8QA
Tel: 020 7739 2266;
www.frizzanteltd.co.uk
Tube: Old Street, then bus

Hackney City Farm is a small-scale working farm set in an urban environment. It's a popular day out for the whole family and children are allowed to get close to the animals. The award-winning on-site café uses only the freshest ingredients for their traditional Italian dishes. The blackboard menu changes every week. Check out the website for recipes, too.

Princess

76 Paul Street EC2A 4NE
Tel: 020 7729 9270
Tube: Old Street

The Australian owners of this attractive gastropub have succeeded in creating a chic, vibrant upstairs dining room. Here they serve hearty fresh food that is skilfully cooked. The menu is inspired by the flavours of the Mediterranean and there is a good list of New World wines.

St John

26 St John Street EC1M 4AY
Tel: 020 7251 0848;
www.stjohnrestaurant.com
Tube: Farringdon

St John is the favourite of many a restaurant reviewer and it is easy to see why. A plain interior doesn't detract attention from Fergus Henderson's revitalising of British dishes. Don't be put off by the famed offal dishes, or Henderson's speciality roast marrow bones, there will always be a dish on the menu that appeals. If you can't get a table, they serve delicious snacks in the bar area, which also has an open bakery. St John Bread and Wine on Commercial Street in Spitalfields sells bread and a hearty breakfast.

Story Deli

3 Dray Walk,
The Old Truman Brewery,
91 Brick Lane E1 6QL
Tel: 020 7247 3137;
www.storydeli.com
Tube: Liverpool Street

The Story Deli prides itself on the fact that every ingredient is organic. The pizza, served from lunchtime onwards, is gaining many fans. The café opens for breakfast and serves food all day. It is a good alternative to the many Indian restaurants here.

Southeast

Many north Londoners say they wouldn't set foot south of the river for love nor money. Ignore them: some parts of southeast London might be bleakly suburban, but there are also places of great interest: the gruesome London Dungeon, inspirational Design Museum and fascinating Royal Observatory and Planetarium to name but a few. And where else, after all, other than maritime Greenwich, can you claim to straddle the world's meridian? This interesting region reaches from London Bridge right along the Thames to Greenwich and, on the opposite side of the river, Canary Wharf. While Greenwich is known for its old-fashioned maritime history, upwardly mobile Canary Wharf, with its New York-style skyscrapers, is the most modern corner of the capital. For bargain hunters, Bermondsey Market, held every Friday, is one of the largest weekly antiques markets in Europe.

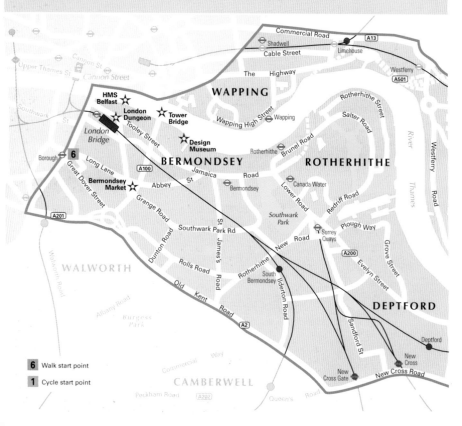

6 Walk start point

1 Cycle start point

NAVAL COLLEGE

CUTTY SARK

West India Quay
Canary Wharf
Canary Wharf
Heron Quays
South Quay

The Dome

Preston's Road

North Greenwich
A102

Millennium Way

ISLE OF DOGS

Manchester Road

East Ferry Rd

Mudchute
Millwall Park
Island Gardens

Blackwall Lane

A206

1

Old Royal Naval College

Vanbrugh Hill

Cutty Sark
Romney Road
Maze Hill

Creek Road

National Maritime Museum

Greenwich Park

Croom's Hill

Greenwich

Royal Observatory & Planetarium

GREENWICH

Blackheath Rd
Blackheath Hill
A2

Unmissable attractions

Appearances can be deceptive: although largely residential, design fans will find much to see in the southeast of London. The area stretches across the Thames from the glass-and-steel skyscrapers of Canary Wharf, the capital's business district with its distinctive Norman Foster-designed tube station, to the parks and buildings of riverside Greenwich, linked by the Docklands Light Railway. Upstream, you don't need to know your Ron Arad from Zaha Hadid to enjoy the Design Museum. One London classic, the sleek tea clipper *Cutty Sark* is due to reopen in 2011 following repairs after a major fire. The ship is currently being tended to in Greenwich.

1 Thames Barrier
The Thames Barrier at Woolwich protects London in the event of a tidal surge that could flood many low-lying areas. It is tested monthly and has been raised almost a hundred times since it was completed in 1982.

2 National Maritime Museum
This is the largest maritime museum in the world and is a landmark in Greenwich. It holds a collection of more than 2 million objects which reflect Britain's historical role as a seafaring nation.

3 London Dungeon
This is easily one of the scariest places to visit in the capital. Even queuing for your ticket can be a claustrophobic experience, so what follows is guaranteed to unsettle you. You can experience the Great Plague and the Fire of London, take the Boat Ride to Hell and see all manner of gruesome events and unpleasant punishments.

4 Design Museum
Exhibitors here are at the cutting-edge of their various fields – architecture, interiors, computing, furniture, shoes, clothing, cars, accessories...The list is exhaustive and the displays and exhibitions are superb.

5 City Hall/GLA Building
Foster and Partners designed this addition to London's riverside for the Mayor, the London Assembly and the Greater London Authority. Completed in 2002, this distinctive glass building is open to the public on weekdays.

BERMONDSEY MARKET
MAP REF TQ333793

Leave Portobello Road Market to the tourists: real antiques hunters wake early on Friday and make their way south of the river to Bermondsey. The market started in the late 1940s and is one of Europe's largest weekly antiques markets. Small items are laid out on the stalls, while larger pieces of furniture are kept in the surrounding warehouses. Bermondsey attracts many professional dealers, so you should aim to arrive early for any bargains.

CANARY WHARF
MAP REF TQ375803

When Canary Wharf tower was under construction sceptics suggested that the shiny new offices there would remain forever unfilled. Who, they asked, would relocate their business to the deprived Isle of Dogs, especially since the Jubilee Line tube connecting Canary Wharf to central London had not been finished? The property crash of the early 1990s seemed to confirm the predictions, but step out of Norman Foster's cavernous Canary Wharf tube station today and you'll be confronted not only by the 800-foot (244m) Canary Wharf tower, but several other sparkling skyscrapers. The docks have been cleaned up, landscaped and surrounded by bars, restaurants and shops. Up to 80,000 people now work at Canary Wharf and thousands shop in the underground mall. You can learn to sail in the docks further down the Isle of Dogs, and the London Triathlon takes place on the roads and waterways. The skyline, while not as awe-inspiring as that of Dubai or many American cities, is a good indication that Canary Wharf is well established as London's centre of business. There are restaurants, health clubs, department stores, luxury car dealers, bars and cinemas. The Docklands Light Railway runs between central London and Greenwich. Take this railway instead of the tube if you want to see Docklands in all its glory. The Museum of London has a Docklands outpost, housed in a 200-year old warehouse on West India Quay. The museum covers the area's history from Roman settlement to trading boom.

DESIGN MUSEUM
MAP REF TQ339799

If your eyes glaze over at fine art and archaeology leaves you cold, then perhaps this is the museum for you. It is the world's first museum dedicated to modern design (the 20th century onwards) and some of the featured designers and special exhibitions are immensely inspiring. The criteria for inclusion are simple: design classics are preferred to design duds, whether they are shoes by Manolo Blahnik, chairs by Arne Jacobsen or cars by Aston Martin. Terence Conran was one of the driving forces behind the conversion of this warehouse, and one of his restaurants, the Blueprint Café, shares the first floor with the Review Gallery of contemporary designs. Due to space limitations the exhibits are changed frequently. The museum runs one of London's best kids' workshops on Sunday afternoons, as well as talks and courses by leaders in fashion, design and architecture.

Bargains in Bermondsey

Borough Market is the last remaining early morning wholesale fruit and vegetable market in central London. Expect to see stalls selling anything from French cheeses and Cumbrian wild boar meat to barbecued burgers and organic vegetables here. Bermondsey Antiques Market operates on Fridays and is altogether different in style and content: the serious dealers have usually completed their trading by 4am. There are plenty of warehouses selling paintings, china, furniture and jewellery.

Route Directions

1 From Borough tube turn left to cross Marshalsea Road and continue along Borough High Street, ignoring the left-hand slip road. A few paces past London Bridge tube is Borough Market. Just after Bedale Road cross the road into St Thomas Street.

2 Take the first right into Great Maze Pond, which runs between the buildings of Guy's Hospital. At the end turn left into Snowsfields. At The Rose pub turn right into Weston Street and continue past the site of the Bermondsey Leather Market, to Long Lane.

3 Turn left and follow Long Lane until you reach some traffic lights. On the right is the Bermondsey Antiques Market. Carry on ahead, then turn right into The Grange. At the end turn left into Grange Road, then first left into Spa Road.

4 Just before the railway arch turn right into Rouel Road and take the first left and go under the railway arch. At the end turn right into St James's Road. Pass the St James Tavern, then turn left on Clements Road.

5 At the end turn right and in about 100yds (91m) turn left into Southwark Park entering though Jamaica Gate. Turn right and follow as the path gently swings to the left; the exit is before the sports complex. Turn left along Hawkstone Road to Surrey Quays tube station.

6 After crossing at the lights take the road behind the station leading into Redriff Road, which then veers left beside the shopping complex.

7 Before the red draw bridge turn right down the steps. At the bottom of the steps turn left following the white sign 'Russia Dock Woodland' and go past a row of town houses beside Greenland Dock. Turn left after the statue of James Walker and, ignoring the first path, turn left under a bridge and continue on the main path to the right. Follow the signs first to 'Ecological Park' and then left to 'Stave Hill'.

8 Take the first right and bear left uphill to Stave Hill. Walk in a clockwise direction to reach the steps to Stave Hill. At the foot of the steps follow the path to Dock Hill Avenue. This crosses two roads before reaching Surrey Water. With this to your left, head for the main road and then turn left and Rotherhithe tube is on the right.

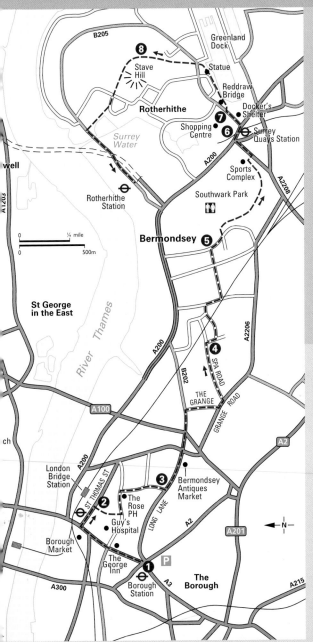

Route facts

DISTANCE/TIME 5.5 miles (8.84km) 3h

MAP AA Street by Street London

START Borough tube station; grid ref: TQ 323797

FINISH Rotherhithe tube station; grid ref: TQ 352798

PATHS Mainly paved streets

GETTING TO THE START Borough tube station is on the Northern line. This is in the congestion charge area and there are no parking facilities.

THE PUB The George, 77 Borough High Street SE1 1NH Tel: 020 7407 2056

HMS BELFAST MAP REF TQ332803

The heavily armoured battle cruiser HMS *Belfast* is now tied up alongside City Hall, but in the Second World War she was patrolling the seas and sinking German warships such as the *Scharnhorst*. Life-size models illustrate what daily life was like for sailors on board and visitors can have a go at targeting the huge six-inch guns. Guides are also on hand to add a little background to the exhibits. Children will seem better suited to the narrow gangways and hatches and they especially enjoy exploring the *Belfast*: weekend activities for families introduce children to other aspects of life at sea.

LONDON DUNGEON

MAP REF TQ331803

For a gruesome, involving and extremely entertaining journey into the depths of London's dungeons just follow the signs from London Bridge station. This top attraction brings death and misery to life with vivid tableaux, hammy acting from guides in period costume and plenty of fake blood. It's not only London's brutal dungeons and the associated torture and executions that are depicted; other low

points in the capital's history, including the Great Plague and the Fire of London, are also covered. Children and the squeamish should approach the London Dungeon with caution.

NATIONAL MARITIME MUSEUM & QUEEN'S HOUSE MAP REF TQ387777

The exploits of British seafarers, from Caribbean pirates to battle-hardened admirals, have shaped the nation and this museum does an excellent job of presenting some of its 2 million exhibits. There's more on show than telescopes, maps and charts: certain sections cover characters such as Admiral Nelson and subjects like astronomy, and there is a planetarium in Neptune Court. Ground-breaking exploration and expeditions are described in fine detail, but there are also displays and film footage of early luxury cruises, plus family-friendly activities for a less intensive visit.

The museum's central building is the Queen's House, a fine royal palace completed in 1635. It is in these splendid surroundings that the National Maritime Museum's art collection is exhibited, including works by Joshua Reynolds, Thomas Gainsborough and J M W Turner, all with a seafaring theme.

■ Activity

HERNE HILL VELODROME

Herne Hill is the world's oldest track cycling circuit and after a few years of uncertainty over its future, it looks like it will play a part in preparing young cyclists for the 2012 Olympics. The outdoor track was the cycling venue for the 1948 Olympics and you can still take a turn around it, although you might not hit the 30mph speeds of professionals. Training sessions offer coaching and bike hire.

OLD ROYAL NAVAL COLLEGE

MAP REF TQ386780

Greenwich can easily occupy a whole day out, but save a bit of time for a visit to this one-time training centre for the Royal Navy. Housed in Sir Christopher Wren's huge and imposing complex of neoclassical buildings, the college has three areas open to the public. The impossibly grand Painted Hall is a vast dining room decorated by artist James Thornhill – it took him 19 years to paint. Look out for the *trompe l'oeil* detailing on the columns and windowsills. The chapel, restored by James Stuart after a fire in 1779, has a superb altarpiece by Benjamin West, *The Preservation of St Paul After the Shipwreck at Malta*. In the Visitor Centre you can survey the busts of various naval heroes before having a break at the Pepys Café. An ice rink is set up outside during the winter months; book in advance.

ROYAL OBSERVATORY & PLANETARIUM MAP REF TQ389772

Greenwich is at the centre of the world – or at least the world's time zones. At the Royal Observatory you can step from one hemisphere to another before exploring the history of both time, space and the scientists who attempted to understand them. It's a fascinating place and well worth visiting, not least for the largest refracting telescope in the country. The Observatory's recent Time galleries explore the roles time and timekeeping play in our daily lives.

TOWER BRIDGE

MAP REF TQ337803

Tower Bridge, which connects the north bank of the Thames at the Tower of London with the south side of the river at the Design Museum, offers those with a head for heights some excellent views along the Thames. The bridge's history – it was completed in 1894 after eight

■ Activity

CITY FARMS

You can hear sheep bleat and the clucking of chickens at excellent city farms where children can intereact with the animls. Mudchute Park and Farm on the Isle of Dogs is overshadowed by the towers of Canary Wharf. Here you see llamas, pet pigs or take horse-riding lessons. Other notable city farms include Hackney City Farm, Vauxhall City Farm and Kentish Town City Farm. Find out more at dwww.visitlondon.com.

■ Visit

RANGER'S HOUSE

This red-brick Georgian villa houses the Wernher Collection, which consists of priceless medieval and Renaissance artworks assembled by 19th-century diamond dealer Sir Julius Wernher. The variety of the items in the collection (including paintings, porcelain, tapestries, jewels and bronzes) adds to its appeal, and you can join one of the behind-the-scenes tours to find out more.

years of construction – and workings are described in the Tower Bridge Exhibition but the highlight for many is the trip along the upper walkways. Those who make it up there get a great view of Norman Foster's environmentally friendly City Hall, the glassy, helmet-shaped home for London's Mayor. The mechanically minded will also enjoy the engine room, although the Victorian cogs and wheels no longer operate the bridge. If possible, try to time your visit for one of the 900 occasions during the year when the bridge is lifted to allow river traffic to pass below.

East from Greenwich along the Thames

In the space of just 3 miles (4.8km) of riverside there is at least a millennium's worth of London's industrial, military and seafaring heritage, from maritime Greenwich, which became the site of the prime meridian in 1884, to the Royal Arsenal at Woolwich, via the Thames Barrier and the O2 Arena. The Thames Barrier has been put to use more than 80 times to protect London from flooding. More than 80 staff operate and maintain the flood defences.

Route Directions

1 From Cutty Sark Gardens wheel your bike along the riverside walk to the Cutty Sark pub and turn right along Ballast Quay, then bear right into Pelton Road. At the Royal Standard pub turn left into Christchurch Way. As you approach the entrance to the Alcatel complex, turn right into Mauritius Road. When you reach Blackwall Lane turn left into the bus lane. Just before the traffic lights take the cycle path on the left along the pavement of Tunnel Avenue. At the footbridge look for the green surfaced track on the left.

2 Cross the footbridge and turn left into Boord Street. At Millennium Way, join the cycle path directly ahead. At West

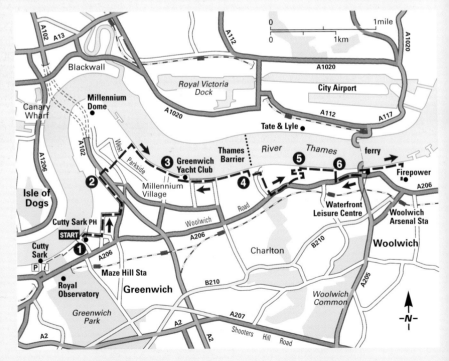

Parkside continue straight on and when you reach the riverside, turn right. Just past the colourful buildings of Greenwich Millennium Village you'll reach the Greenwich Peninsula Ecology Park.

3 The outer boardwalk is always open and considerate cyclists are welcome. Go on along the riverside path, which turns inland to skirt the Greenwich Yacht Club's fenced enclosure. Remain on the riverside past the aggregate recycling works. At the end of that section, stay on the street called Riverside, with the large Sainsbury's depot to your right. Look out for the remains of old dockside railway tracks on your left. At Anchor and Hope Lane take the off-road path to go straight ahead.

4 On reaching the Thames Barrier, the green-surfaced route around the complex is well-signed and quite easy to follow. At the former Thames Barrier Arms pub, go straight ahead along the path which is slightly overgrown and quite narrow. There is a steep slope up to the crossing at Woolwich Church Street. Turn left along the road here and when you reach the roundabout, take the second exit (Ruston Road). Look for the left turn where

Ruston Road heads towards the river. Turn left here and turn left again at Harlinger Road. When you reach the T-junction turn right, then right once again.

5 A sign asks cyclists to dismount for the 40yd (37m) section between the road and the riverside. When you rejoin the riverside opposite the Tate & Lyle works on the north bank, turn right. When the pedestrian route uses steps to cross a wall, the cycle path heads inland, where you will find a ramp, and returns to the riverside.

6 At the cannons on the riverside turn inland past the Clockhouse Community Centre. At Leda Road make your way up the slope to join Woolwich Church Street. You may prefer to dismount and push your bike along the pavement to reach the Woolwich free ferry. At the Ferry Approach look for the cycle signs by the ambulance station. Pass the Waterfront Leisure Centre and the entrance to the Woolwich Foot Tunnel. Continue along the riverside to Royal Arsenal Pier, where a large piazza provides access to the revitalised Royal Arsenal complex, including the Firepower Museum. From

Route facts

DISTANCE/TIME 6 miles (9.7km) 2h

MAP AA Street by Street London

START/FINISH The Cutty Sark pub, Ballast Quay; grid ref: TQ389782. Pay parking at Cutty Sark Gardens

TRACKS Largely surfaced cycle lanes, some cobbled streets

GETTING TO THE START The Cutty Sark pub is northeast of the centre of Greenwich. Lassell Street leads to Ballast Quay from Trafalgar Road (A206). On-street metered parking is limited to 2 hours; Greenwich Council underground parking at Cutty Sark Gardens is a short walk or cycle ride.

CYCLE HIRE None available locally

THE PUB The Cutty Sark, 4–7 Ballast Quay SE10 9PD Tel: 020 8858 3146

❶ This ride includes some busy on-road sections where you may prefer to dismount.

here it is possible to cycle inland to explore the shops, pubs and restaurants of Woolwich centre before you cycle back to Greenwich.

■ PLACES OF INTEREST

Bermondsey Market
Bermondsey Square SE1
3UN. Tube: Bermondsey.

Britain at War Experience
Churchill House,
64–66 Tooley Street SE1 2TF
Tel: 020 7403 3171;
www.britainatwar.co.uk
Tube: London Bridge.

Canary Wharf
Docklands, E14.
Tube: Canary Wharf.

Cutty Sark
King William Walk SE10 9HT
Tel: 020 8858 2698;
www.cuttysark.org.uk
Tube: Cutty Sark DLR,
Greenwich DLR.

Design Museum
28 Shad Thames SE1 2YD
Tel: 020 7403 6933;
www.designmuseum.org
Tube: London Bridge,
Tower Hill.

Dulwich Picture Gallery
Gallery Road SE21 7AD
Tel: 020 8693 5254; www.
dulwichpicturegallery.org.uk
Train: North or West Dulwich.

Fashion and Textile Museum
83 Bermondsey Street
SE1 3XF. Tel: 020 7407 8664;
www.ftmlondon.org
Tube: London Bridge.

HMS *Belfast*
Morgan's Lane, Tooley Street
SE1 7JH. Tel: 020 7940 6300;
www.iwm.org.uk
Tube: London Bridge,
Tower Hill.

Horniman Museum
100 London Road SE23 3PQ
Tel: 020 8699 1872;
www.horniman.ac.uk
Train: Forest Hill.

London Dungeon
28–34 Tooley Street SE1 2SZ
Tel: 020 7403 7221;
www.thedungeons.co.uk
Tube: London Bridge.

**Museum of London
in Docklands**
No.1 Warehouse, West India
Quay, Canary Wharf E14 4AL
Tel: 020 7001 9844; www.
museumindocklands.org.uk
Tube: Canary Wharf
Train: West India Quay

National Maritime Museum
Romney Road SE10 9NF
Tel: 020 8858 4422;
www.nmm.ac.uk
Tube: Cutty Sark DLR,
Greenwich DLR.

Old Royal Naval College
Greenwich SE10 9LW
Tel: 020 8269 4747; www.
oldroyalnavalcollege.org
Tube: Cutty Sark DLR,
Greenwich DLR.

Queen's House
Romney Road SE10 9NF
Tel: 020 8858 4422;
www.nmm.ac.uk.
Tube: Cutty Sark DLR,
Greenwich DLR.

Ranger's House
Chesterfield Walk SE10 8QX
Tel: 020 8853 0035;
www.english-heritage.org.uk
Train: Blackheath.

**Royal Observatory
& Planetarium**
Greenwich Park SE10 9NF
Tel: 020 8858 4422;
www.nmm.ac.uk
Tube: Cutty Sark DLR,
Greenwich DLR.

Tower Bridge
SE1 2UP. Tel: 020 7403 3761;
www.towerbridge.org.uk
Tube: Tower Hill.

■ SHOPPING

Greenwich Market
Greenwich Market,
Greenwich SE10 9HZ
www.greenwichmarket.net
Train: Greenwich Station,
Cutty Sark Gardens
It celebrated its 25th
anniversary in 2010, and
this covered market
continues to offer an eclectic
selection of goods.

Montblanc
Canada Place, Canary Wharf
E14 5AH. Tel: 020 7719 1919;
www.montblanc.com
Tube: Canary Wharf.
Sells Montblanc's collection
of elegant fountain pens,
watches and jewellery.

Mudchute Park and Farm
Pier Street, Isle of Dogs
E14 3HP. Tel: 020 7515 5901;
www.mudchute.org
Train: Crossharbour
This city farm is home to 200
animals and there's always
something for adults and
children to do. Free.

Le Pont de la Tour Food Store
Butler's Wharf Building,
36 Shad Thames SE1 2YE
Tel: 020 7403 8403;
www.conran.com
Tube: Tower Hill.
The Butler's Wharf building
lures gourmets with its
Conran restaurants
(wonderful modern French
cuisine) and tempting food
stores, such as this glorious
delicatessen, selling cheese,
pâté and olive oils.

Zara
Cabot Place West, Canary
Wharf E14 4QT
Tel: 020 7715 1970
Tube: Canary Wharf
Affordable women's and
men's clothing from a retailer
with its finger on the pulse.

▓ ACTIVITIES

Brockwell Lido
Dulwich Road SE24 0PA.
Tel: 020 7274 3088;
www.lambeth.gov.uk
Train: Herne Hill.
Modernised lido at the foot of
Brockwell Park.

Docklands Sailing and Watersports Centre
235a Westferry Road,
Isle of Dogs E14 3QS.
Tel: 020 7537 2626;
www.dswc.org
Tube: South Quay DLR.
Learn how to sail, row, canoe
or even powerboat with the
Royal Yachting Association
at this leading watersports
centre in London.

Herne Hill Velodrome
Burbage Road SE24 9HE
www.hernehillvelodrome.com
Train: Herne Hill.
Contact Vélo Club de Londres
at www.vcl.org.uk/hernehill/
for coaching and bike hire.

▓ GREEN SPACES

Centre for Wildlife Gardening
28 Marsden Road, East
Dulwich SE15 4EE
Tel: 020 7252 9186;
www.wildlondon.org.uk
Train: East Dulwich.
How to make your garden
more attractive to animals.
Dulwich Common
SE21 7LE
Train: West Dulwich.

Greenwich Park
Blackheath Gate,
Charlton Way SE10 8QY
Tel: 020 8858 2608;
www.royalparks.gov.uk
Tube: North Greenwich.
The oldest Royal Park in
London has a small herd of
deer and stupendous views.

▓ PERFORMING ARTS

The O2 Arena
Greenwich Peninsula
SE10 0DX. Tel: 0844 056 0202;
www.theo2co.uk
Train: North Greenwich
A state-of-the-art concert
venue with a nightclub,
cinema and eateries.

Up the Creek
302 Creek Road SE10 9SW
Tel: 020 8858 4581;
www.up-the-creek.com
Train: Greenwich.
This comedy club confronts
stand-up comedians,
experienced or fresh-faced,
with a raucous crowd.

▓ EVENTS

Great River Race
Island Gardens, Greenwich.
www.greatriverrace.co.uk
Up to 300 waterborne craft
participate in this race down
the River Thames in late
summer; the finish line is just
beyond Canary Wharf at
Island Gardens.

Greenwich and Docklands International Festival
www.festival.org.
This multi-faceted festival
takes place in various forms
across southeast London in
early summer. Performances
can be spectacular.

London Marathon
Greenwich Park.
www.london-marathon.co.uk
For some, it might be an
ordeal they'd prefer to forget,
but this annual run, walk or
hobble in April attracts more
than 40,000 participants and
hundreds of thousands of
spectators. It starts from
Greenwich Park.

Blueprint Café

Design Museum, Shad
Thames SE1 2YD
Tel: 020 7378 7031;
www.danddlondon.com
Tube: Tower Hill
The views from here are the
best in the area and the daily
changing menu, described
as Modern European, offers
adventurous dishes such as
ox tongue with beetroot and
horseradish; prices reflect
the fine cooking. Dine on the
terrace in summer.

Butler's Wharf Chop House

Butler's Wharf Building,
36e Shad Thames SE1 2YE
Tel: 020 7403 3403;
www.danddlondon.com
Tube: Tower Hill
British cuisine gets a real
makeover here. The menu is
weighted towards the British
classics such as lemon sole
or roast rib of beef, but done
with a light touch. The lunch
deals offer excellent value
and there's a good choice of
wines by the glass.

Franklins

157 Lordship Lane SE22 8HX
Tel: 020 8299 9598;
www.franklinrestaurant.com
Train: East Dulwich.
In the vicinity of Dulwich
Common, Franklins is a
highly regarded suburban

restaurant. It prides itself on
its traditional dishes – from
breadcrumbed skate to roast
grouse, with old-fashioned
steamed pudding and custard
for dessert – made from only
British ingredients. The wine
list includes a few reasonably
priced bottles.

The Gun

27 Coldharbour E14 9NS
Tel: 020 7515 5222;
www.thegundocklands.com
Tube: Canary Wharf
With a sleek, monochrome
interior, decorated with
antique muskets and rifles,
the Gun gastropub touts for
business from the workers
at nearby Canary Wharf. It's
a wonderful place for a drink,
thanks to the views across
the Thames to the Dome,
but the food and service can
be hit and miss.

The Old Brewery

Old Royal Naval College
Greenwich SE10 9LW
Tel: 020 3327 1280; www.
oldbrewerygreenwich.com
Train: Cutty Sark
The latest project of brewer
Alastair Hook, founder of
Greenwich's Meantime
Brewery, has been to return
a working brewery to the
grounds of the Old Royal
Naval College. Restaurant
and bar food is served in the

spectacular, historic space,
dominated by the eight
copper stills of the
microbrewery. But many will
be be happy to savour a pint
of Meantime's best and take
in the surroundings.
Meantime's own pub in
Greenwich, the Greenwich
Union at 56 Royal Hill, is a
TV-free spot to enjoy Hook's
London-influenced porters
and ales.

Trafalgar Tavern

Park Row SE10 9NW
Tel: 020 8858 2909;
www.trafalgartavern.co.uk
Tube: Cutty Sark DLR,
Greenwich DLR
The Trafalgar is one of the
more upmarket eateries in
Greenwich. The paintings and
prints on the walls have an
appropriately maritime feel,
but the real attractions are
a selection of good ales and
outdoor riverside seating.

Wagamama

Jubilee Place,
45 Bank Street E14 5NY
Tel: 020 7516 9009;
www.wagamama.com
Tube: Canary Wharf
This branch of the successful
chain, Wagamama, is the
largest in the country. It
offers the usual super-quick
service at communal tables.
The menu is also unchanged.

South Bank & South

The South Bank runs between London Bridge and Lambeth Bridge and in this compact corner of London you'll find the most successful millennium attraction, the London Eye. The neighbourhood of Borough often passes for 18th-century London on film and television, or you can step back in time still further – 400 years – at Shakespeare's Globe theatre. Children will love the London Aquarium, while art fans won't want to miss the monumental Tate Modern to the east. It's possible to cover most of the South Bank on foot – or you can take a boat instead.

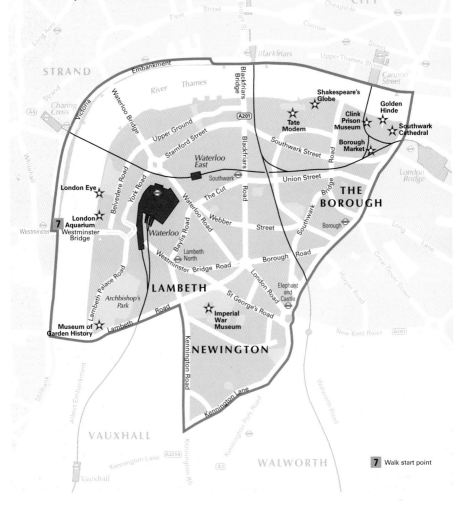

7 Walk start point

GOLDEN JUBILEE WALKWAY

Unmissable attractions

The South Bank packs a potent hit of history, culture and sightseeing. This is where William Shakespeare's plays were performed in the original Globe Theatre and where film directors use the 18th-century alleys of Borough marketplace to shoot period films. At weekends the market halls are packed with Londoners shopping for fresh produce. As Borough Market attracts foodies, so Tate Modern is a beacon for modern art lovers and the London Eye is a hit with tourists and Londoners alike.

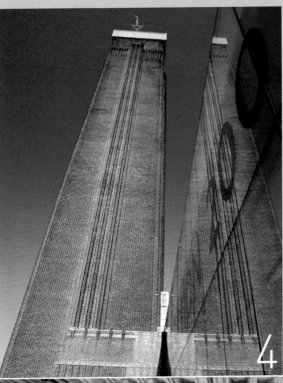

1 **London Eye**
Now one of London's most popular attractions, the Eye offers a leisurely overview of the sights.

2 **Gabriel's Wharf**
A collection of speciality shops and restaurants is gathered together here on the South Bank.

3 **Shakespeare's Globe**
Soak up the atmosphere of a 17th-century-style play at the Globe.

4 **Tate Modern**
Fantastic modern art in an industrial, spacious and airy setting.

5 **Southwark Cathedral**
This Gothic cathedral is near the river and historic alleys and lanes.

BOROUGH MARKET

MAP REF TQ326802

When Borough Market isn't being used as a film location (scenes from the Harry Potter films and crime caper *Lock, Stock and Two Smoking Barrels* were shot here), it is a gastronomic paradise on Fridays and Saturdays.

It was only when farmers' markets caught the public imagination in recent years that Borough Market opened to the public. Now, there are 70 stallholders selling excellent, if expensive, produce. Gastronomica sells Italian charcuterie and cheeses, while Scandelicious offers Scandinavian foods. Butchers, bakers and coffee merchants also trade at Borough Market and a visit is highly recommended for foodies. The best time to explore the alleyways of the 18th-century marketplace is on Friday afternoon, when all the stallholders have arrived and the celebrity chefs are checking out the week's produce, but before the place becomes swamped on Saturday morning.

When you've finished shopping, the Market Porter opposite the entrance arch is one of the best places in London for a pint of beer.

CLINK PRISON MUSEUM

MAP REF TQ326803

Parts of Southwark pass for Dickensian London in television adaptations; follow the steps down from street level to Clink Prison and you enter a far gloomier world of gruesome punishments and wretched prisoners. Clink Prison (hence 'in the clink') opened in the 12th century and was owned by successive bishops of Winchester until the 18th century, when it was burned down during rioting. Prisoners incarcerated at Clink included prostitutes, thieves, adulterers and debtors. At various times, Protestants and then Catholics were imprisoned here for their beliefs.

Today, you can experience what inmates went through at this small basement museum, which explains the history of the prison and details some of the punishments meted out. Torture was common: you could be stretched on the rack, broken on the wheel or crushed under heavy weights. In 1530, King Henry VIII decreed that women who were unfaithful to their husbands could be boiled in oil. For less serious crimes, such as selling goods under the correct weight, you could be put in the stocks and pillories, flogged or even ducked under water.

GOLDEN HINDE

MAP REF TQ326803

The most surprising thing about the *Golden Hinde* is its diminutive size. After all, this is a full-size replica of the ship that Sir Francis Drake sailed around the world between 1577 and 1580. It makes his epic journey all the more amazing to know that the 70-foot (21m) galleon would have been manned by 80 sailors, living and working on the five decks. This replica was launched in 1973 and has also been sailed around the world. It is now moored a few steps from Southwark Cathedral.

There is not much information explaining how the ship works, so a guided tour is a good idea.

A walk along the River Thames, following its bridges

Westminster Bridge was built in the 1740s. More than a hundred years later, the Hungerford Bridge, the only combined rail and foot crossing, extended the railway line into Charing Cross. Work began to replace Waterloo Bridge in 1939 and took six years. The present Blackfriars Bridge has five cast-iron arches. Millennium Bridge is the newest crossing and the latest London Bridge is a 20th-century structure.

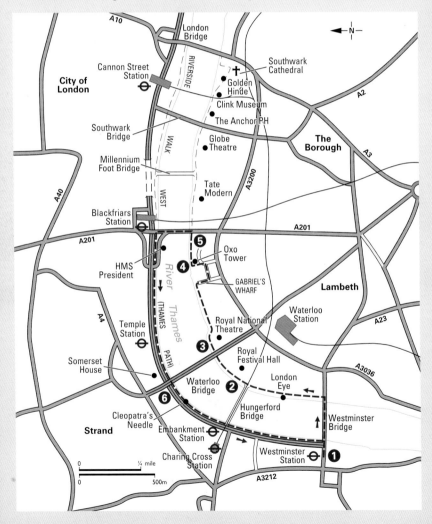

Route Directions

1 Leave Westminster tube station by Exit 1 to follow signs to Westminster Pier. Walk up the steps to your right and cross Westminster Bridge. Turn left along the riverfront. Ahead are the 32 transparent pods of the 2,100-ton London Eye, a huge modern ferris wheel. Just past Jubilee Gardens, on the right, is the next bridge, Hungerford, sandwiched between two newer pedestrian bridges called the Golden Jubilee Bridges.

2 Continue ahead past the Royal Festival Hall and look to the opposite bank of the Thames for Cleopatra's Needle. After the National Film Theatre and its outdoor café is Waterloo Bridge.

3 The path bends to the right, past the Royal National Theatre and the Hayward Gallery, before reaching the craft shops and restaurants of Gabriel's Wharf. Turn right at the Riviera restaurant and walk through the central path lined on either side with a series of wooden sculptures. Turn left at the end into Stamford Street and 100yds (91m) further on take another left turn into Barge House Street.

4 Ahead, the brown brickwork of the Oxo Wharf somewhat shrouds the entrance to the Oxo Tower. Enter the glass doors to your left and catch the escalator to the eighth floor for a view of the skyline, or continue along the ground floor to the riverside exit.

5 Cross Blackfriars Bridge and turn left to follow the Thames Path along the wide pavement adjacent to the river. The first boat you will pass on your left is the HMS *President*. The next set of buildings to your right after Temple tube station belong to the University of London. Immediately after these comes majestic Somerset House.

6 A further 200yds (183m) ahead the path passes Cleopatra's Needle before reaching Embankment tube. Northumberland Avenue is the next road to appear on your right. About 200yds (183m) further on is Horse Guards Avenue, which is sandwiched between the formidable buildings of the Old War Office and the Ministry of Defence. You are now almost parallel with the London Eye, on the opposite bank of the River Thames. When you reach Westminster Bridge turn right into Bridge Street, to Westminster tube and the start.

Route facts

DISTANCE/TIME 2.75 miles (4.4km) 1h15

MAP AA Street by Street London

START/FINISH Westminster tube station; grid ref: TQ 302797

PATHS Paved streets and riverside walk

GETTING TO THE START Westminster tube station is on the Circle, Jubilee and District lines. This is in the congestion charge area and there are no parking facilities.

THE PUB The Anchor, 34 Park Street, Bankside, London SE1 9EF Tel: 020 7407 1577

❶ Keep any children well supervised as this is a riverside walk.

IMPERIAL WAR MUSEUM

MAP REF TQ314791

The Imperial War Museum succeeds in its brief of covering conflicts involving Britain or the Commonwealth without sentimentality or jingoism. It presents the apparatus, art and aftermath of war with a combination of scholarly gravity and an instinct for what will interest and intrigue visitors. In the soaring Large Exhibits Gallery, which opens the collection, fighter planes, including a Spitfire, are suspended above tanks, boats and submarines. Many of the exhibits have stories of heroism attached to them, while others impress through the sheer sense of scale: how did Second World War pilots squeeze into those tiny cockpits? The behind-the-scenes exhibits in the ground-floor galleries surrounding the main room are even more engaging. There are recreations of the Blitz and trench warfare, while on the second floor you can enter the world of the spy. The next floor offers a selection of work from some of the best-known war artists, such as John Singer Sargent, Paul Nash and Stanley Spencer. But it is the permanent Holocaust Exhibition that provides the numbing counterpoint to the martial display below. The minutiae of death are chilling, while the filmed testimony of Holocaust survivors is very moving. The exhibition is not thought suitable for under-14s.

LONDON AQUARIUM

MAP REF TQ307798

Learn to tell a conger eel from a moray eel at the London Aquarium, one of Europe's largest aquariums. The 50 displays are arranged according to 14 of the world's watery habitats, with the Atlantic Ocean exhibit forming the centrepiece. Sharks and stingrays patrol the inside of this three-storey tank and are hand-fed by divers daily. There are 350 species in total at the aquarium and many visitors, children especially, develop a soft spot for the rays, which seem to enjoy being petted at the Touch Pool. However, the tanks with the most eye-catching residents are the Coral Reef and Indian Ocean displays, which contain species seriously endangered by overfishing and global warming. Other habitats include tropical freshwater, rivers, ponds, mangroves and rainforest waterways, where you will find catfish, pufferfish and – to the relief of the tank's other inhabitants – a species of piranha (vegetarian!) called pacu. Other species on show include starfish and jellyfish.

LONDON EYE MAP REF TQ307799

It was a publicity coup without equal. In the millennial flurry of new projects and buildings, the London Eye, to the surprise of most observers, stole the show from the Millennium Dome. Its popularity with Londoners and visitors alike has ensured that the wheel will continue turning on its central site opposite the Houses of Parliament for the foreseeable future.

So, what's the appeal of a 450-foot (137m) big wheel? It's not just the breathtaking views across the capital; views that even on a cloudy day stretch along the Thames to Canary Wharf and on a clear day can extend up to 25 miles

(40km). And it's more than admiration for a feat of engineering that keeps 32 space-age glass pods suspended on a giant bicycle wheel of cables, girders and tubes for your half-hour revolution. No, it is perhaps the sheer novelty of seeing some of the world's most recognisable landmarks, such as Buckingham Palace, from the air.

The Eye is extremely popular during the summer and booking ahead is advised, especially if you're confident of picking a fine day. In the darker winter months there are special night-time 'flights'.

MUSEUM OF GARDEN HISTORY MAP REF TQ306790

Since reopening in 2008, the Museum of Garden History has delighted green-fingered visitors with its exhibitions and visiting lecturers while providing a tranquil green space in which to gather one's thoughts. Close to Lambeth Palace (and opposite the Houses of Parliament), it's still a surprise to find fragrant flowerbeds, trimmed hedges and neat lawns on the South Bank. Tips on inner-city gardening are forthcoming from the museum's experts and banana and olive trees offer proof of London's mild microclimate. The history part of the museum ranges from tools and ceramics to books and paintings. But it's the museum's enviable events calendar that is the secret of its success. There's something going on every weekend, from festivals of herbs or wildflowers to talks from celebrity gardeners. And you can get your hands dirty with regular workshops and activities.

■ Insight

MILLENNIUM BRIDGE

For several years after its construction, Norman Foster's elegant Millennium Bridge was known as the 'Wobbly Bridge'. When it opened in 2000 it swayed under the footfall of people crossing the Thames so it was swiftly closed for alterations. The improved bridge reopened in 2002 and remains the most enjoyable – and stable – way of walking between two of London's stand-out attractions, St Paul's Cathedral and Tate Modern.

SHAKESPEARE'S GLOBE
MAP REF TQ322805

This is the brainchild of American actor Sam Wanamaker and was completed in 1997. It is a reconstruction of the theatre where William Shakespeare debuted many of his plays and is a must-see attraction, thanks in large part to Wanamaker's insistence on building the new Globe theatre only with tools, materials and techniques available in Elizabethan times (displays explain the construction process in detail). The original Globe was opened in 1599, but the circular, wooden playhouse burned down shortly afterwards. Not only does the new Globe look fantastic but, during the summer performance season, you can see Shakespeare's work in as authentic a setting as possible. The season normally runs from May to October and the open-air stage means favourable weather is an advantage. It's standing room only in the pit in front of the stage but there are seats for those with less stamina. It was a favourite Elizabethan custom for the 'groundlings'

in the pit to heckle the actors, and today the audience is still essential to every performance. The Globe provides back-to-basics drama, with no elaborate sets or props: Shakespeare's words and the building create their own magic.

SOUTHWARK CATHEDRAL
MAP REF TQ327804

Glowing with the brightness of cleaned and restored stonework, Southwark Cathedral may not look like one of London's oldest Gothic buildings, but it is. The cathedral was a simple priory church (dating from the 13th century) until 1905, when the diocese of Southwark was formed and the church became upgraded to a cathedral. You'll find a monument and window dedicated to William Shakespeare in the south aisle and the tombs of Bishop Lancelot Andrews, translator of the King James version of the Bible, and John Gower, an English poet who died in 1408. On the north side of the nave a stained-glass window depicts people associated with Southwark and the cathedral, including preacher John Bunyan and Geoffrey Chaucer, who started his pilgrimage to Canterbury from the Tabard Inn, just off nearby Borough High Street. The Long View of London museum, a garden and a refectory are recent additions.

TATE MODERN MAP REF TQ320804
Tate Modern is simply the most important gallery of modern art in Britain. But despite a collection that includes some of the biggest names of the 20th century – Henri Matisse, Pablo Picasso, Andy Warhol and Francis Bacon

– the art can be dwarfed by the towering architecture of the converted Bankside power station. The Tate Modern building, unmistakable at the south end of the Millennium Bridge, began life in the 1950s as a power station, designed by the man who also came up with Britain's distinctive red telephone boxes, Giles Gilbert Scott. After the power station was decommissioned, the Swiss architectural firm Herzog & de Meuron was charged with transforming the brick-and-steel frame building into a home fit for the Tate Gallery's ever-increasing collection of modern art.

There are two entrances to Tate Modern, at the west and north sides. Both lead into the awe-inspiring Turbine Hall, a vast space that lends itself to whatever monumental sculptures or installations are placed in it. The galleries are spread around the spacious upper levels. In 2006, Tate Modern rehung its collection around the new themes of Abstract Expressionism, Cubism, Minimalism and Surrealism, following criticism that the original organisation according to themes of landscape or history was too subjective and vague. Artists Anish Kapoor and Roy Lichtenstein now have works displayed for the first time at Tate Modern. Other artists, including Juan Muñoz, Thomas Schütte and Mark Rothko have rooms to themselves. There are still extensive seasonal exhibitions at the gallery. One experience you shouldn't miss is a well-earned break in either the café on level two or the more expensive top-floor restaurant – both serve good food and offer excellent views over the Thames.

■ PLACES OF INTEREST

Borough Market
8 Southwark Street SE1 1TL
Tel: 020 7407 1002;
www.boroughmarket.org.uk
Tube: London Bridge.

Clink Prison Museum
1 Clink Street SE1 9DG
Tel: 020 7403 9000;
www.clink.co.uk
Tube: London Bridge.

Golden Hinde
St Mary Overie Dock,
Cathedral Street SE1 9DE
Tel: 020 7403 0123;
www.goldenhinde.org
Tube: London Bridge.

Imperial War Museum
Lambeth Road SE1 9HZ
Tel: 020 7416 5000;
www.iwm.org.uk
Tube: Lambeth North.

London Aquarium
County Hall, Westminster
Bridge Road SE1 7PB
Tel: 0871 663 1678;
www.sealife.co.uk/london
Tube: Waterloo, Westminster.

London Eye
County Hall, Riverside
Building, Westminster Bridge
Road SE1 7PB
Tel: 0870 500 0600;
www.ba-londoneye.com
Tube: Waterloo, Westminster.

Millennium Bridge
Tube: Blackfriars, St Paul's,
Southwark.

Museum of Garden History
Lambeth Palace Road
SE1 7LB
Tel: 020 7401 8865;
www.gardenmuseum.org.uk
Tube: Lambeth North,
Waterloo

Shakespeare's Globe
21 New Globe Walk SE1 9DT
Tel: 020 7902 1500;
www.shakespeares-globe.org
Tube: London Bridge,
Southwark.

Southwark Cathedral
London Bridge SE1 9DA
Tel: 020 7367 6700;
www.southwark.anglican.org/
cathedral
Tube: London Bridge.

Tate Modern
Bankside SE1 9TG
Tel: 020 7887 8888;
www.tate.org.uk
Tube: St Paul's, Southwark.

■ SHOPPING

Annie Sherburne
Unit 1.10 Oxo Tower Wharf
Bargehouse Street SE1 9PH
Tel: 020 7922 1112;
www.anniesherburne.co.uk
Tube: Blackfriars, Waterloo.
Annie Sherburne specialises
in eco-friendly products, from
reclaimed and restored
vintage items.

Bankside Gallery
48 Hopton Street SE1 9JH
Tel: 020 7928 7521;
www.banksidegallery.com
Tube: Southwark.
The home of the Royal
Watercolour Society and the
Royal Society of Painter-
Printmakers. Most works on
display are for sale.

D'Argent
Unit 1.01 Oxo Tower Wharf
Bargehouse Street SE1 9PH.
Tel: 020 7401 8454;
www.dargentonline.co.uk
Tube: Blackfriars, Waterloo
Jewellery designer Louise
Sherman exhibits her designs
and other work in this shop.
Bespoke designs, in gold and
silver, can be commissioned.
The wharf's independent
businesses are supported by
the Coinstreet Community
Trust and you can find them
all at www.coinstreet.org.

Konditor & Cook
22 Cornwall Road SE1 8TW
Tel: 020 7261 0456
Tube: Waterloo.
10 Stoney Street SE1 9AD
Tel: 020 7407 5100
www.konditorandcook.com
Tube: London Bridge.
Both branches of this
patisserie sell delectable
cakes, fruit tarts, breads and
pastries. Although there is no
seating, they're excellent
places to buy lunch.

Neal's Yard Dairy
6 Park Street, Borough
Market SE1 9AB
Tel: 020 7367 0799;
www.nealsyarddairy.co.uk
Tube: London Bridge.
An outpost of Covent
Garden's famous shop
stocking seasonal cheeses.

Southbank Printmakers Gallery

12 Gabriel's Wharf SE1 9PP
Tel: 020 7928 8184; www.
southbank-printmakers.com
Tube: Southwark.
Limited-edition etchings, woodcuts, lithographs and linocuts.

W2 Products

Unit 1.22, Oxo Tower Wharf, Barge House Street SE1 9PH
Tel: 020 7922 1444;
www.w2products.com
Tube: Blackfriars, Waterloo.
W2 stocks English Heritage's Blue Plaque collection, including tea towels and bone china mugs.

■ GALLERIES & ENTERTAINMENT

BFI Southbank

South Bank SE1 8XT
Tel: 020 7928 3535;
www.bfi.org.uk/nft
Tube: Embankment, Waterloo.
The best venue in the city for art-house movies.

Hayward Gallery

Belvedere Road SE1 8XZ
Tel: 020 7921 0813;
www.southbankcentre.co.uk
Tube: Waterloo.
Some of London's most exciting exhibitions of contemporary art.

IMAX Cinema

1 Charlie Chaplin Walk
SE1 8XR. Tel: 08700 787 2525;
www.bfi.org.uk/imax
Tube: Waterloo.
The cinema is accessed by underground walkways. The screen is the UK's largest.

National Theatre

South Bank Centre SE1 9PX
Tel: 020 7452 3000;
www.nationaltheatre.org.uk
Tube: Embankment, Waterloo, Southwark.
The National offers fresh takes on old classics, as well as new plays and exhibitions of photography.

Old Vic

Waterloo Road SE1 8NB
Tel: 0844 871 7628;
www.oldvictheatre.com
Tube: Waterloo.
The Old Vic's artistic director is actor Kevin Spacey.

Purcell Room

South Bank Centre SE1 8XX
Tel: 020 7921 0813;
www.rfh.org.uk
Tube: Embankment, Waterloo.
Solo performances, chamber music and contemporary music recitals.

Queen Elizabeth Hall

South Bank Centre SE1 8XX
Tel: 020 7921 0813;
www.southbankcentre.co.uk
Tube: Embankment, Waterloo.
Small orchestral concerts, operas and piano recitals.

Royal Festival Hall

South Bank Centre SE1 8XX
Tel: 020 7921 0813;
www.southbankcentre.co.uk
Tube: Embankment, Waterloo.
The base for the London Philharmonic Orchestra, as well as the Philharmonia and the London Sinfonietta. There are frequent classical performances in the 3,000-seat hall.

Young Vic

66 The Cut SE1 8LZ
Tel: 020 7922 2922;
www.youngvic.org
Tube: Southwark, Waterloo.
Leading stage for younger directors and artists.

■ SPORTS & ACTIVITIES

The London Bicycle Hire Company

1a Gabriel's Wharf SE1 9PP
Tel: 020 7928 6838;
www.londonbicycle.com
Tube: Southwark.
Bicycles and helmets are available for hire.

Sustrans

www.sustrans.org
If you have rented a bike or have one of your own, follow some of the Sustrans routes around London. National Route 4 passes along the South Bank as it links Hampton Court in the west to Greenwich in the east. You can download maps from the website to help you follow the signposted routes.

Anchor & Hope
36 The Cut SE1 8LP
Tel: 020 7928 9898
Tube: Southwark, Waterloo
This gastropub is the stand-out place to eat in the streets between Waterloo and the river. You can pick single dishes, such as the house speciality of duck hearts on toast, or larger roasts to be shared among friends. You may have to wait for a table.

Baltic
74 Blackfriars Road
SE1 8HA
Tel: 020 7928 1111;
www.balticrestaurant.co.uk
Tube: Southwark
This sleek, brightly lit place serves food loosely derived from the countries around the Baltic: expect starters such as marinated herring salad with apple, beetroot and sour cream and mains such as chargrilled lamb shashlik with Georgian salad and flatbread. The bar stocks a huge variety of flavoured vodkas, best drunk with blinis to take the edge off.

Magdalen
152 Tooley Street SE1 2TU.;
Tel: 020 7403 1342;
www.magdalenrestaurant.co.uk
Tube: London Bride
Chefs David Abbott and James and Emma Faulks source many of their ingredients for Magdalen's hearty dishes from nearby Borough Market. Seasonality is prized and the emphasis is on slow-cooked traditional dishes such as marrow bone with toast. The wine list is a highlight.

The Market Porter
9 Stoney Street SE1 9AA
Tel: 020 7407 2495
Tube: London Bridge
The Market Porter is nirvana for beer lovers. Opposite Borough Market, it is often ranked as one of London's best pubs because it has up to 30 different guest beers every month. Favourites include brews from Archer's and Harvey's but regulars are not slow to try out the more obscure beers on offer. The pub also serves basic meals, such as sausages and mash, in an upstairs dining room.

Oxo Tower Brasserie
Oxo Tower Wharf, Barge House Street SE1 9PH
Tel: 020 7803 3888
Tube: Blackfriars, Waterloo
Turn right out of the lift at the rooftop of the Oxo Tower for the brasserie and bar; a left turn will lead you to the altogether pricier restaurant, but the superb views across the Thames are the same from either. The starters trot across the globe from sashimi of tuna with ginger and mirin dipping sauce to slow-braised osso bucco.

The Royal Oak
44 Tabard Street SE1 4JU
Tel: 020 7357 7173
Tube: Borough
Flock wallpaper, plastic ashtrays and green tiles: yes, this is a traditional London pub that remains unspoiled and blithely untroubled by the gastropub renovators. Excellent ales supplied by an independent Sussex brewery called Harvey's are the main reason to visit the Royal Oak. The Royal Oak serves traditional pub food; Sunday's main attraction is a full roast lunch followed by a traditional sherry trifle.

Tapas Brindisa
18–20 Southwark Street
SE1 1TJ
Tel: 020 7357 8880
Tube: London Bridge
This hugely popular tapas bar on the corner of Stoney Street is invariably full to bursting with people enjoying acorn-fed Iberian ham, gambas and other Spanish specialities. Arrive early to secure a table because there is a no-booking policy.

Baroque

VICTORIA AND ALBERT MUSEUM

West & Southwest

Although some of the world's costliest real estate lies in Kensington and Chelsea, there are some surprisingly affordable pleasures to be had here: you can ride round Hyde Park on a horse or bicycle, or learn all about medicinal plants in Chelsea Physic Garden. But the real bargains are the three world-class museums in South Kensington: the Natural History Museum, the Science Museum and the Victoria & Albert Museum. Of course, Harvey Nichols and Harrods are ready to help if you simply want to have a fun afternoon of quality retail therapy.

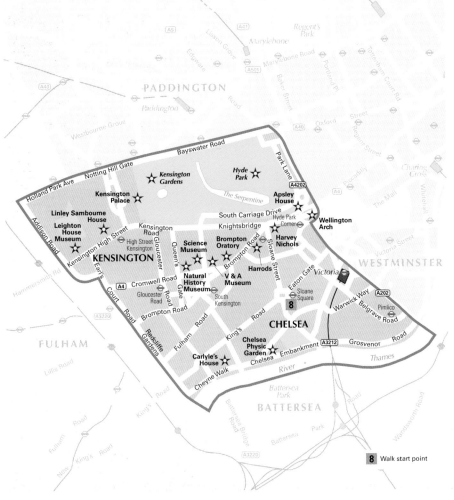

8 Walk start point

DIANA FOUNTAIN, HYDE PARK

ALBERT MEMORIAL

Unmissable attractions

Chelsea, Kensington and Knightsbridge are some of the swankiest areas of London, but that doesn't mean that there aren't some treats for free. Among the genteel streets of South Kensington are three of the capital's most enthralling museums: the Victoria & Albert Museum, the Natural History Museum and the Science Museum, where entry is always free. Next, you can cover some of Chelsea's highlights – including the Chelsea Physic Garden and Carlyle's House – on foot. Finally, you can burn off whatever energy you have left in the 350-acre (142ha) Hyde Park. It's up to you whether you explore it on foot, bicycle, rollerblades or horseback.

1 Natural History Museum
The main entrance to the museum leads into the central hall with this popular dinosaur exhibit.

2 Knightsbridge
The excellent shops to be found in this area of London include the world's most famous department store, Harrods.

3 Victoria & Albert Museum
The V&A celebrates the history of the decorative arts up to the present. Its collections are huge so take time to explore.

4 Science Museum
Accessible science and technology for all. As well as excellent displays, the exhibitions are wonderful.

5 Hyde Park's Rotten Row
This broad. tree-lined avenue in Hyde Park has always been a popular trotting place for London's horse-riders.

APSLEY HOUSE
MAP REF TQ284798

There is no shortage of grand 18th-century town houses in London, but what sets Apsley House apart is that it belonged to the remarkable Arthur Wellesley, the Duke of Wellington. The Duke not only lent his name to the eponymous rubber boot, defeated Napoleon at the Battle of Waterloo in 1815 and became Prime Minister in 1928, he was also an avid collector of art. Paintings, porcelain, sculpture and furniture are all part of his collection, displayed in the splendid Regency rooms of Apsley House. The house itself was known as No.1 London because it was the first property encountered after passing through the city's western toll gates in Knightsbridge. The Wellesley family still lives in the part of the house which is not open to the public, and in fact this is the only English Heritage property in which the original owner's family still lives.

BROMPTON ORATORY
MAP REF TQ272792

The Oratory, next to the Victoria & Albert Museum, is an Italian baroque church, the second-largest Catholic church in the country. While the Oratory's exterior dominates its surroundings, it's the ornate interior that takes your breath away. The nave and dome are decorated with Giuseppe Mazzuoli's 17th-century marble statues, gilded columns and vivid paintwork. Despite the busy southwest London location, it manages to retain some tranquillity. The centrepiece of the church is the Italian marble altarpiece, featuring cherubs floating on marbled clouds. Mass is held here on Sunday mornings and is quite an experience, with High Latin chanting, angelic choristers and frankincense swirling from the swinging censer.

CARLYLE'S HOUSE
MAP REF TQ272776

Thomas Carlyle was a Scottish historian, philosopher and satirist who lived in this four-storey terraced house with his wife, Jane, from 1834 to 1881. The house itself dates from 1708 and, unlike many others in Cheyne Row, remains almost unchanged since the 19th century. The Carlyles never owned the property and, in contrast to the cost of houses on this sought-after London street today, paid only £35 in rent – at that time Chelsea was an unfashionable area in which to live. Carlyle completed his first book, *Sartor Resartus*, two years before relocating to London. The success of the book ensured that he was a popular and influential figure in the 19th-century arts world and 24 Cheyne Row became a gathering place for Victorian literary society. Among the visitors were the poets Alfred Tennyson, Robert Browning and Matthew Arnold. Carlyle was also

■ Insight

BROMPTON CEMETERY
Brompton Cemetery, unconnected to the Oratory and further down Old Brompton Road to the west, is the only cemetery managed by the Royal Parks service. It's not morbid and the 35,000 headstones include many elaborate Victorian tombs. There are regular guided walks.

friends with the philosopher John Stuart Mill and writer and critic John Ruskin. Mill disagreed with many of Carlyle's opinions and the two drifted apart, but Carlyle was an important influence on Ruskin and also Charles Dickens. While literary visitors will be enthralled by this rich background, you don't have to be a bookworm to appreciate the Victoriana of Carlyle's house, such as the Queen Anne furniture and many of Carlyle's personal possessions. He spent a lot of his time in the garret, trying to find as much peace and quiet as possible, although it was in his drawing room that he died in 1881.

CHELSEA PHYSIC GARDEN
MAP REF TQ277778

You'll have to time your visit to Chelsea Physic Garden carefully: it is open only Wednesday to Friday and Sundays and Bank Holidays from April through to October. But the wait is worth it because the garden is not only of interest from a scientific and medical point of view, it is also a surprisingly serene place to catch your breath. The Physic Garden dates from 1673, when it was established to teach students about plants. This, of course, was a time when new plants and cuttings were being brought back to London on ships that had travelled the globe. Its south-facing site on the bank of the Thames was chosen for its temperate climate, in the hope that many of the exotic specimens would survive – one such attraction is Britain's largest outdoor fruiting olive tree. By the 18th century, the garden had set up an international botanic seed exchange system, which continues today. Most of the garden's plants, numbering some 5,000 species, have medicinal properties. Within the Physic Garden, the Garden of World Medicine is Britain's first garden of ethnobotany and there is also a Pharmaceutical Garden. Other corners are devoted to perfume, aromatherapy and vegetables. For more of an insight into the garden's history, guides are on hand to show visitors around, but it is just as rewarding to wander among the unusual shrubs, trees and plants before venturing back to the King's Road.

HARRODS MAP REF TQ276794

The world's most famous department store, Harrods plays the grande dame to Harvey Nichols' young pretender. Its terracotta bricks, deep green livery and doormen – now sufficiently relaxed to let those wearing jeans inside the store – are instantly recognisable the world over. Although the store is showing its age (it opened in 1849) many of the halls are still spectacular temples to ostentatious consumption. The tiled food halls in particular should be on the must-visit list of any shopper. Most of the leading fashion designers have concessions here; the clothing ranges become more youth-orientated the higher up the building you go. But, unless you care to scramble for a place in the winter sale, there aren't many bargains to be had. The annual sale remains legendary for its queues and the hype. Most serious shoppers conduct pre-sale sorties to work out the quickest route to their targets, but for a general browse around the floors, it is best to avoid opening day.

Chelsea

Chelsea is home to the most famous pensioners in Britain. They live in The Royal Hospital, founded by Charles II in 1692 for veteran soldiers. The minimum age is 65 and there is still accommodation for 500. Chelsea Pensioners surrender their army pension in return for a small room, all meals, clothing and medical care. They are easily recognised by their unusual three-cornered hats and their scarlet coats.

Route Directions

1 From Sloane Square tube walk ahead, crossing Lower Sloane Street. Go past Peter Jones and, a few paces

on your left, the Duke of York Square. Turn left into Cheltenham Terrace then bear left into Franklin's Row.

2 Turn right on the Royal Hospital Road. Just beyond the lawns on the right, turn left into the hospital grounds

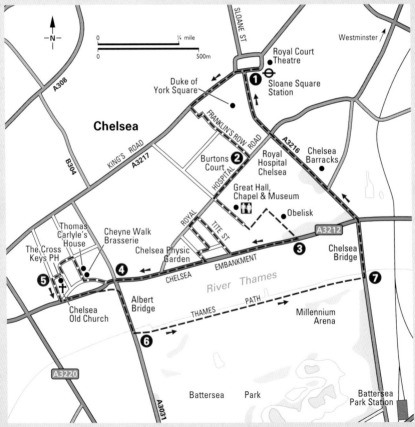

at Chelsea Gate. (A few paces further on the left, a gravel path leads to the Great Hall, chapel and museum.) Continue to the end of the road and turn left on to some playing fields. Now head towards the obelisk, bear right and leave through the gates to the Chelsea Embankment.

3 Turn right along the Embankment and right into Tite Street, where Oscar Wilde once lived. At Royal Hospital Road turn left into Paradise Walk. The houses in this narrow, quiet road have window boxes and roof terraces. Turn right and then sharp left towards the Embankment and walk past the Chelsea Physic Garden.

4 At the Albert Bridge traffic lights cross Oakley Street and bear right along the narrow Cheyne Walk. Turn right by the Cheyne Walk Brasserie into Cheyne Row, where Thomas Carlyle lived. At the end turn left into Upper Cheyne Row. Turn left again into Lawrence Street – where there is a plaque to mark the Chelsea Porcelain Works – then turn right into Justice Walk. (Don't be fooled into thinking the sign of a red-robed judge is a pub, it merely

identifies where the old courthouse used to be!)

5 Turn left into Old Church Street and at the bottom is Chelsea Old Church, with a statue outside of Thomas More, who worshipped here. Walk through Chelsea Embankment Gardens and cross the Albert Bridge.

6 At a 'Riverside Walk' sign turn left through the gate into Battersea Park. Follow the Thames Path, past the Peace Pagoda in the park, along to Chelsea Bridge.

7 Turn left to cross the bridge and continue ahead, passing Chelsea Barracks on the right before joining Lower Sloane Street. Turn right to retrace your steps back to Sloane Square tube station.

Route facts

DISTANCE/TIME 3.75 miles (6km) 2h

MAP AA Street by Street London

START/FINISH Sloane Square tube station; grid ref: TQ 281787

PATHS Paved streets and tarmac paths

GETTING TO THE START Sloane Square tube station is one stop west from Victoria station on the District line. This is in the congestion charge area and there are no parking facilities.

THE PUB The Coopers Arms, 87 Flood Street, London SW3 5TB Tel: 020 7376 3120.

❶ Sections of the walk are close to the river; keep children supervised.

HARVEY NICHOLS

MAP REF TQ278797

A short walk towards Hyde Park from Harrods, the ever-fashionable Harvey Nichols trumps its retail rival on several fronts. First, there's the Fifth Floor restaurant, a well-regarded eatery with superb views and only one of several in-store eating options. Second, Harvey Nichols' buyers tend to bring in less well-known designers and fresh brands, which makes for a more interesting and eclectic shopping experience. Of course, you'll still find big names. As well as the clothing ranges, Harvey Nichols also has a strong line-up of on-the-spot beauty treatments, with manicures, facials and revitalising massages all available to footsore and weary shoppers.

HYDE PARK MAP REF TQ274804

Hyde Park, which adjoins Kensington Gardens, is central London's largest royal park. Although the flat landscape verges on the featureless, there are interesting sights to find. Since Henry VIII bought the park in 1536 it has been the setting for some of London's dramas. Refugees from the slums camped in the park in 1655 in the hope of escaping from the Great Plague. The park was at the heart of disturbances in 1866 between the police and the Reform League, and since 1872 people have been permitted to speak freely at Speaker's Corner to the northwest. The park has become a convenient venue for large-scale open-air concerts. It's also a much-appreciated space for Londoners to get some exercise on bicycles and rollerblades. Both skaters and bladers congregate at Hyde Park Corner for a regular Friday-night skate, while cyclists are allowed on the park's roads but not its paths. Other sporting activities include impromptu games of football and softball, while the Tennis Centre allows non-members to turn up and play. Runners are a common sight and summer sees swimmers take to the water of the Serpentine at the Lido.

KENSINGTON PALACE & GARDENS MAP REF TQ258801

Kensington Palace, where she lived, will forever be closely associated with Diana, Princess of Wales. Flowers are still left tied to the black-painted gates to the Gardens on the anniversary of her death, while inside a collection of her dresses forms one of the permanent exhibitions. There's more to Kensington Palace and Gardens than its most famous resident. The Royal Ceremonial Dress Collection spans three centuries of regal finery, with the whole process of designing and fitting a dress explained. Upstairs the his-and-hers State Apartments include the understated Queen's Apartment and the over-the-top King's Apartment, where Queen Victoria was baptised. In the gardens, the Orangery is a sublime, elegant space in which to have lunch before exploring the gardens. The Sunken Garden is a highlight. However, it won't take you long to find the Serpentine Gallery to the south and the garden's two sculptures: *Physical Energy* and *Peter Pan*. This just leaves the Albert Memorial on the southern edge of the gardens, a magnificent tribute to Queen Victoria's beloved husband.

Visit

SERPENTINE GALLERY

The gallery is known for bold, challenging exhibitions and projects. Among these is the annual summer pavilion, which is commissioned from leading architects such as Rem Koolhaas, Daniel Libeskind and Oscar Niemeyer. The pavilion is used for activities and events and the gallery also hosts family days throughout the year.

LEIGHTON HOUSE MUSEUM

MAP REF TQ248793

Red-brick Leighton House was built to the owner Lord Frederic Leighton's own specification in 1864–66. Leighton was a widely travelled artist and illustrator – he ventured to the Middle East, North Africa and all over Europe – before he settled in this Holland Park house. You can see the influence of his travels throughout the interior. Leighton was an enthusiast of the Pre-Raphaelite movement and many pieces from his Pre-Raphaelite collection are in the museum. Leighton House Museum builds on Leighton's love of art and schedules a wide range of events during the year.

LINLEY SAMBOURNE HOUSE MAP REF TQ252794

You can guess Linley Sambourne's occupation from the cartoonist's work which covers the walls of his house. Sambourne lived here from 1874 to 1910 and the Italianate terraced townhouse has been preserved almost as he left it. Most of the décor remains from the late Victorian period and you get a unique glimpse into the life of an upwardly mobile household through the collection of 135,000 bills, letters and diary pages. A guided tour reveals even more about the family and the times in which they were living. Families are welcome on the daytime tours – the house is open at weekends from March to December – but it is adults only for the evening tour, which includes a glass of wine.

NATURAL HISTORY MUSEUM MAP REF TQ267791

Where else can you see frighteningly realistic animatronic dinosaurs? Or experience the scary tremors of an earthquake? The museum does an excellent job of engaging with younger visitors via the use of interactive or multimedia displays such as the Ant Colony, an army of leafcutter ants, or the Power Within room, in which the effects of the 1995 Kobe earthquake are replicated. Mostly, however, the exhibits don't need any help to enthrall: the creepy crawlies are a perennial favourite and the dinosaur skeleton takes pride of place in the cavernous central hall of the Life Galleries. The Natural History Museum holds special exhibitions and regular talks and events.

In 2009, to celebrate the 200th anniversary of Charles Darwin's birth, an eight-storey extension, the Darwin Centre, was opened. This hive of activity houses 17 million insects and some of the museum's 220 scientific staff, who you can watch at work.

SCIENCE MUSEUM

MAP REF TQ268792

The Science Museum is practically next door to the Natural History Museum and is similarly successful at stimulating children – thanks to its broad and liberal interpretation of the word science, which manages to include classic computer games and 3D films.

The collections cover the stories behind many of the world's most important inventions: Babbage's Calculator, Stephenson's *Rocket* and Arkwright's Spinning Jenny. The full-size replica of the Apollo 10 command module is a highlight. On the first floor Who Am I? investigates the human brain and psychology, while the exhibition on power in the East Hall explores the past and future of energy. As well as all the interactive computers and exhibits, there's a daily programme of IMAX film screenings and events, including the Science Night Sleepover for parties of six or more.

V&A MUSEUM MAP REF TQ269792

The third in South Kensington's trio of world-class museums will mesmerise anyone interested in art, culture or society. The V&A's field is the decorative arts, but through this subject it manages to traverse continents and centuries of human history. The best plan of action is to savour just one or two collections at a time. Highlights include the Fashion, Jewellery and Accessories collection, which displays fashionable dress from the 17th century to the present day. The Furniture and Furnishings collection consists of 14,000 items from the Middle Ages onwards, while the Ceramics collection is central to the museum. It includes everything from Egyptian relics to modern industrial ceramics via porcelain, such as the Meissen vulture acquired in 2006. During school holidays and on most weekends there are activities for families. There are also several trails around the museum for children aged 7–12 to follow. Best of all, the museum's Back-Packs scheme allows children to borrow one of a series of themed backpacks and use the contents to explore different subjects. You don't need to book. For adults, the V&A stays open late every Friday and on the last Friday of the month it hosts themed extravaganzas, often involving music, talks and even dressing up.

WELLINGTON ARCH
MAP REF TQ285798

Decimus Burton's arch was built in 1830 to celebrate the Duke of Wellington's victories over Napoleon's armies. The statue of the Duke on horseback that topped the arch was replaced before the First World War with a 38-ton bronze sculpture, the heaviest in Europe, called *Peace Descending on the Quadriga of War*, depicting four war horses and the Angel of Peace. There are three floors of displays; carry on to the top of the arch and take in the spectacular views of Buckingham Palace from the balcony.

■ Insight

KING'S ROAD
King's Road may have lost some of its sparkle since the swinging 1960s, but few streets are better for a Saturday afternoon meander. Yes, it will be crowded, but half the fun of window-shopping is watching other people. There are plenty of cafés and the shops get more interesting the further you walk from Sloane Square.

■ PLACES OF INTEREST

Apsley House
149 Piccadilly W1J 7NT
Tel: 020 7499 5676;
www.english-heritage.org.uk
Tube: Hyde Park Corner.

Brompton Oratory
Brompton Road
SW7 2RP
Tel: 020 7808 0900;
www.bromptonoratory.com
Tube: South Kensington.

Carlyle's House
24 Cheyne Row SW3 5HL
Tel: 020 7352 7087;
www.nationaltrust.org.uk
Tube: Sloane Square.

Chelsea Physic Garden
66 Royal Hospital Road
SW3 4HS
Tel: 020 7352 5646; www.
chelseaphysicgarden.co.uk
Tube: Sloane Square.

Harrods
87–135 Brompton Road
SW1X 7XL
Tel: 020 7730 1234;
www.harrods.com
Tube: Knightsbridge.

Harvey Nichols
109–125 Knightsbridge
SW1X 7RJ
Tel: 020 7235 5000;
www.harveynichols.com
Tube: Knightsbridge.

Hyde Park
W2 2UH
Tel: 020 7298 2100;
www.royalparks.gov.uk
Tube: Hyde Park Corner,
Knightsbridge.

Hyde Park
& Kensington Stables
63 Bathurst Mews Lancaster
Gate, W2 2SB
Tel: 020 7723 2813;
www.hydeparkstables.com
Tube: Lancaster Gate.

Kensington Palace
& Gardens
Kensington Gardens W8 4PX
Tel: 0844 482 7777;
www.hrp.org.uk
Tube: Bayswater, High Street
Kensington.

King's Road
Tube: Sloane Square.

Leighton House Museum
12 Holland Park Road
W14 8LZ. Tel: 020 7602 3316;
www.rbkc.gov.uk
Tube: High Street Kensington.

Linley Sambourne House
18 Stafford Terrace W8 7BH
Tel: 020 7602 3316;
www.rbkc.gov.uk
Tube: High Street Kensington.

Natural History Museum
Cromwell Road SW7 5BD
Tel: 020 7942 5000;
www.nhm.ac.uk
Tube: South Kensington.

Science Museum
Exhibition Road SW7 2DD
Tel: 0870 870 4868;
www.sciencemuseum.org.uk
Tube: South Kensington.

Serpentine Gallery
Kensington Gardens W2 3XA
Tel: 020 7402 6075;
www.serpentinegallery.org
Tube: Lancaster Gate.

V&A Museum
Cromwell Road SW7 2RL
Tel: 020 7942 2000;
www.vam.ac.uk
Tube: South Kensington.

Wellington Arch
Hyde Park Corner W1J 7JZ
Tel: 020 7930 2726;
www.english-heritage.org.uk
Tube: Hyde Park Corner.

■ SHOPPING

& Clarke's
122 Kensington Church
Street W8 4BU
Tel: 020 7229 2190;
www.sallyclarke.com
Tube: Notting Hill Gate.
Follow your nose to Sally
Clarke's bakery for breads,
patisserie, and other treats.

Austique
330 King's Road SW3 5UR
Tel: 020 7376 3663;
www.austique.co.uk
Tube: Fulham Broadway,
Sloane Square.
Pretty partywear, jeans and
hard-to-find labels are the
speciality of this women's
clothing boutique.

Hummingbird Bakery
133 Portobello Road
W11 2DY
Tel: 020 7229 6446; www.
hummingbirdbakery.com
Notting Hill's famous bakery
pre-empted the cupcake
trend in 2004. One cookbook
later and the Hummingbird
has gone global. Get a taste

of the cheerfully retro cakes and the famous cupcakes for a sugar hit like no other.

Lulu Guinness

3 Ellis Street SW1X 9Al.
Tel: 020 7823 4828;
www.luluguinness.com
Tube: Sloane Square.
Lulu Guinness's bags are a favourite of label lovers.

Peter Jones

Sloane Square SW1W 8EL.
Tel: 020 7730 3434;
www.peterjones.co.uk
Tube: Sloane Square.
The store has had a makeover and is attracting younger shoppers.

Snow and Rock

188 Kensington High Street W8 7RG.
Tel: 020 7937 0872;
www.snowandrock.com
Tube: High Street Kensington.
Fantastic selection of outdoor clothing and equipment.

Urban Outfitters

36–38 Kensington High Street W8 4PF
Tel: 020 7761 1001;
www.urbanoutfitters.co.uk
Tube: High Street Kensington.
The latest denim and street fashions from the first of the American chain's shops.

■ ACTIVITIES

Chelsea Football Club

Stamford Bridge,
Fulham Road SW6 1HS
Tel: 0871 984 1955;

www.chelseafc.co.uk
Tube: Fulham Broadway.
You'll need to book well ahead for matches here.

Serpentine Lido

Hyde Park W2 2UH
Tel: 020 7706 3422;
www.serpentinelido.com
Tube: Knightsbridge.
The Lido is open from June to September for swimming and sunbathing.

Twickenham Stadium

Rugby House, 21 Rugby Road, Twickenham TW1 1DS
Tel: 020 8892 2000;
www.rfu.com
Train: Twickenham.
Rugby Union's main stadium.

■ GREEN SPACES

Battersea Park

www.batterseapark.org
Train: Battersea Park
The park has been returned to its Victorian layout. There's also an art gallery to explore.

■ EVENTS

BBC Sir Henry Wood Promenade Concerts

Royal Albert Hall,
Kensington Gore SW7 2AP
Tel: 020 7589 8212;
www.bbc.co.uk/proms
Tube: Knightsbridge, South Kensington.
Better known as the Proms, this series of summer concerts sees performances from top musicians.

Chelsea Flower Show

Royal Hospital,
Royal Hospital Road
SW3 4SR
Tel: 020 7649 1885;
www.rhs.org.uk
Tube: Sloane Square.
Get your tickets early.

London to Brighton Veteran Car Run

From Hyde Park.
www.lbvcr.com
Tube: Hyde Park Corner.
Annual outing to Brighton.

■ PERFORMING ARTS

Bush Hall

310 Uxbridge Road
W12 7LJ
Tel: 020 8222 6955;
www.bushhallmusic.co.uk
Tube: Shepherd's Bush.
Bijou venue for classical and acoustic concerts.

Royal Albert Hall

Kensington Gore
SW7 2AP
Tel: 020 7589 3203;
www.royalalberthall.com
Tube: South Kensington.
Classical concerts and other major events.

Shepherd's Bush Empire

Shepherd's Bush Green
W12 8TT. Tel: 020 83543300;
www.02shepherdsbush
empire
www.02shepherdsbush
empireco.uk
Tube: Shepherd's Bush.
Great for rock and pop acts.

Bibendum

Michelin House,
81 Fulham Road SW3 6RD
Tel: 020 7581 5817;
www.bibendum.co.uk
Tube: South Kensington
Bibendum is a chic,
French-style restaurant
housed in an impressive art
deco building. Although the
fixed menu is good value,
there are two other options
for a quick bite to eat: the
Bibendum Oyster Bar in
the foyer and the Coffee Bar
at the front.

Bluebird

350 King's Road SW3 5UU
Tel: 020 7559 1000;
www.danddlondon.com
Tube: Sloane Square
Chef Mark Block takes
British cuisine seriously in
this swanky, glass-fronted
restaurant. However, for
more palatable prices, the
associated Bluebird Café and
Courtyard is a better bet,
serving breakfasts, snacks
and takeaways.

The Grenadier

18 Wilton Row SW1X 7NR
Tel: 020 7235 3074
Tube: Hyde Park Corner
The Grenadier, helpfully
identified by a red sentry box
and as many hanging baskets
as the Chelsea Flower Show,
is a pub of the old school: the
400-year-old bar dispenses
beer and Bloody Marys while
the restaurant serves an
old-fashioned selection of
quite pricey dishes. Close to
Harvey Nichols and Harrods.

Hereford Road

3 Hereford Road W2 4AB
Tel: 020 7727 1144;
www.herefordroad.org
Tube: Bayswater, Queensway
Since opening in 2007,
Hereford Road has carved
a reputation for excellent,
honest food and a convivial
atmosphere. Fittingly, the
venue used to be a butcher
and the chef is a protégée of
St John's Fergus Henderson
so expect robust, meaty
dishes sourced from British
producers. The set lunch is
particularly good value.

Petersham Nurseries Café

Petersham Road TW10 7AG
Tel: 020 8605 3627; www.
petershamnurseries.com
Tube: Richmond
If you've come all the way to
Richmond Park, this is an
ideal place to break your
journey. The café at the
Nurseries has a reputation
that reaches way beyond its
rickety tables. The reason?
The café's policy of using
only high-quality seasonal
produce, from small UK
producers and farms. Make
sure you stop off at the shop.

River Café

1a Station Approach, Fulham
SW6 3UH. Tel: 020 7736 6296
Tube: Putney Bridge
No, not that River Café
of Jamie Oliver fame: this
small, family-owned café
is an architectural gem and
worth the trip just to see
a traditional, 1950s-style
London 'caff' with formica
tables, tiles and a busy
counter over which snacks,
sandwiches and hot drinks
are served to locals. There's
street-side seating when
the classic interior gets
too packed.

Tom's Kitchen

27 Cale Street,
Chelsea SW3 3QP
Tel: 020 7349 0202;
www.tomskitchen.co.uk
Tube: South Kensington
Sandwiched between the
Fulham Road and King's
Road, Tom Aiken's brasserie
serves breakfast, lunch and
dinner plus a very popular
brunch at the weekend. The
emphasis is on favourites
– eggs Benedict, burgers and
risottos – given a gourmet
twist. The prices also have
a Chelsea twist but the open
kitchen, wood-fired oven and
interior compensate.

North & Northwest

From Regent's Park and up to the hills of Hampstead via Camden and west to Notting Hill, this area contains some of London's most fashionable neighbourhoods and boutiques. Today's celebrities are not the first to settle here: the houses of John Keats and Sigmund Freud are open to the public. But there are some low-key delights here too: take a wildlife walk on Hampstead Heath; a ride on a narrowboat at Little Venice or enjoy an evening at an open-air concert at Kenwood House. Active types can try rock climbing or go swimming in freshwater ponds.

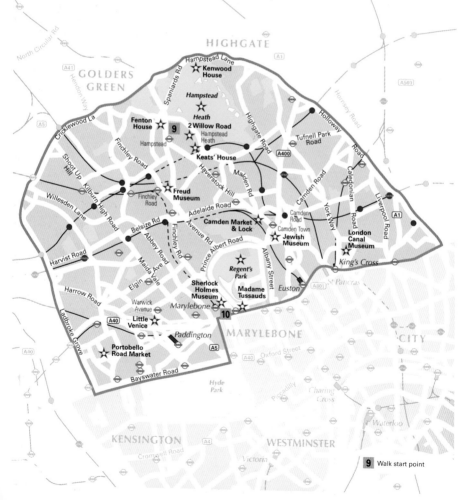

9 Walk start point

PRIMROSE HILL

MADAME TUSSAUDS

Unmissable attractions

Hip, quaint, crowded or spacious, northwest London has a split personality. To the south, Notting Hill entices celebrity spotters and shoppers alike with Portobello Road's boutiques and weekend market. Farther north, Hampstead Heath is one of London's wildest areas, with freshwater ponds, wildlife-spotting walks and even open-air concerts in the gardens at Kenwood House. Between the two, narrowboats chug along the remnants of London's network of canals, which culminate in the secluded corner of Little Venice. Stretches of the canal border Regent's Park, famous for a rose garden, its fine café and more exotic wildlife in ZSL London Zoo.

4

5

1 Primrose Hill
The name applies to the fashionable district as well as the hill to the north of Regent's Park. The hill itself is a popular leisure destination for families.

2 ZSL London Zoo
A meerkat on guard at his enclosure. Renovations have added a children's zoo, Animal Adventure, with a watery play area, and Rainforest Life, showing life during the day and night of a rainforest. Larger animals like the elephants have already been relocated to Whipsnade.

3 Portobello Market
This is one of the most famous markets in the city. It has appeared in television programmes and films and is thronged with visitors most days. There might not be many bargains, but just soak up the atmosphere.

4 Little Venice
As you would expect from the name, this is an area of waterways bordered by shops and restaurants. It is possible to walk along the tow path from here to Camden Market.

5 Hampstead
The Hill Garden and Pergola on West Heath are a delight. They are busy at weekends, but make a wonderful spot for a walk or just a place to sit a while and enjoy the views.

CAMDEN MARKET & CAMDEN LOCK MAP REF TQ286842

A visit to Camden Market is still a rite of passage for many teenagers, but it is overwhelmed with tourists these days and isn't always quite the cutting-edge shopping experience it once was. If you keep walking away from Camden Town tube station and the original market (on your right), you'll reach Camden Lock where the High Street crosses Regent's Canal and the small area of 200 shops and stalls here is much more promising. Clothing, jewellery and music are the main business for traders, although some also sell antiques and homeware. Funky clothing from young designers is also on offer at the Stables Market, which is farther up Chalk Farm Road and closer to Chalk Farm tube station. The Stables is a semi-permanent setting for vintage clothing shops in the Gin House area and furniture and antiques dealers in the Horse Hospital. In total there are about 350 outlets in the Stables Market, including numerous stalls selling foods and produce from all over the world.

FENTON HOUSE
MAP REF TQ263859

Fenton House, a 17th-century red-brick building on the north side of Hampstead Heath, makes for an enchanting day out. It is open from spring to autumn, the perfect time to take a stroll through the rambling old walled garden. Inside the house, collections of early musical instruments (such as 17th-century harpsichords) and European ceramics paint a delightful picture of the life of the prosperous 18th-century merchant who lived here. If you are musically inclined you can audition to play some of the instruments by writing in advance. Concerts are staged in the summer, and egg hunts take place at Easter.

FREUD MUSEUM
MAP REF TQ265848

Sigmund Freud, known as the father of psychoanalysis, moved into this large Hampstead house in 1938, and his family lived there until 1982. Today it is an interesting and intimate museum. The most famous exhibit is Freud's couch, draped in a luxurious rug from Iran. Also in the study – the core of the museum – are some of Freud's antiques and many of his books (when the family fled from Austria before the Second World War they brought most of their possessions to London). Sigmund Freud's daughter Anna was a noted child psychiatrist, and there is also an exhibition of her work.

HAMPSTEAD HEATH
MAP REF TQ273868

Hampstead Heath is the largest green space in north London and it has a less 'managed' feel than London's royal parks. Thanks to being to allowed to run a little wild, it is now one of London's most welcoming habitats for wildlife and there are bird-watching and bat-spotting walks. Parts of the Heath have been designated Sites of Special Scientific Interest (SSSI) and, with some careful nurturing, habitats such as old-growth woodland, bogs and even rare heathland have begun to thrive. But most people will associate Hampstead Heath with its ponds. There are 25 of them, but the

Highgate Ponds for bathing are on the east side, off Millfield Lane. There are separate freshwater ponds for men and women and they are a liberating and sociable way to cool down on a hot August afternoon. Towards the south of the Heath, Parliament Hill Lido offers more facilities. It had a refurbishment in 2005 and there are now better filters and fewer leaks. Close to the Lido there is an athletics track, though most recreational runners will prefer to jog on the Heath itself, among the horse-riders, cyclists, walkers and kite-flyers. Other sports include cricket and tennis, and there are new facilities to cater for volleyball and pétanque players. However, the real highlight of Hampstead Heath is its elevated vantage point – from Parliament Hill you can look out across London landmarks.

JEWISH MUSEUM

MAP REF TQ288837

The recently extended Camden branch of the Jewish Museum (there is another in Finchley) contains a superb collection of Jewish ceremonial art that exemplifies the Jewish principle of *hiddur mitzvah* or beautifying the commandment. The centrepiece is a painted synagogue ark from 17th-century Venice. The museum specialises in English silverwork and there are some beautiful Torah scrolls, candlesticks and goblets. Spread over two galleries, the long history of Jews in Britain is covered. One outstanding exhibit is Percy Levy's *Book of Life*, a collection of childhood memories of the early 20th century. Another treasure trove is the photographic collection with

■ Activity

BAT WALKS
During the summer months the London Bat Group holds nocturnal bat walks on Hampstead Heath. They are an opportunity to learn more about these intriguing mammals and are very popular. Several bat species live on Hampstead Heath, including Daubenton's bat, which hunts for insects near water, and the noctule bat, one of the largest species in Britain, with a wingspan of up to 16 inches (40cm).

captivating images of Jewish theatres, workplaces and family life. The museum holds regular talks and events, with workshops and family events scheduled for Jewish holidays.

KEATS HOUSE MAP REF TQ271857

The quintessential Romantic poet John Keats lived in this white-fronted house in Hampstead from 1818 to 1820. His neighbour was Fanny Brawne, with whom he fell in love and who inspired some of the poetry he composed in the two years he lived here. Keats moved to the house to escape the pollution of London and often walked on Hampstead Heath with Fanny. But it was in the garden at Wentworth Place, as the house was known, that he composed his famous *Ode to a Nightingale*. Much of the furniture in the house is original, and both house and garden are open to the public all year round. Regular literary events and poetry readings are held there. Keats travelled to Rome in the hope of improving his health, but died there from TB at the age of only 25.

Hampstead

A walk on sprawling Hampstead Heath, just 4 miles (6.4km) from central London, is the perfect escape from city life. Hampstead first became fashionable in the 18th century, when the discovery of spring water transformed the village into a Georgian spa town. Writers, poets and painters were attracted by the open space and healthy aspect. This is so today, although the only spring water you'll find is sold in bottles.

Route Directions

1 Turn left outside Hampstead tube along Hampstead High Street and left into Flask Walk. Continue down the

hill past Burgh House and Hampstead Museum, along Well Walk and past Wellside on the right. Cross East

Heath Road and continue along the heath path.

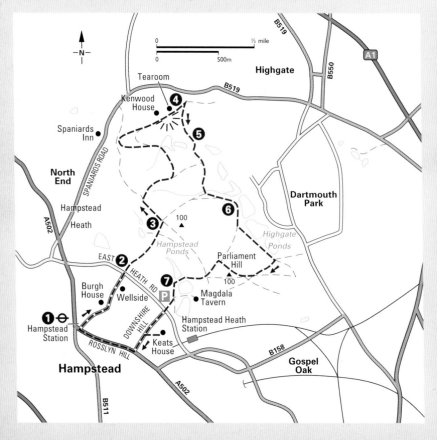

2 Follow a tree-lined path past a fingerpost and a water tap and then after 100yds (91m) turn left at a crossing of paths by a bench. At a fork, bear left and soon afterwards turn right to go through a gate indicating the entrance to the 112 acres (45ha) maintained by English Heritage's Iveagh Bequest.

3 Turn left and bear left as the path descends gently through woodland. If you have a dog it should be on a lead now. Keep ahead to cross a bridge over a lake. Kenwood House can be seen over to the right. Turn left and keep along a path that sweeps round, passing to the right of the house along a wide terrace that overlooks grassland. The Spaniards Inn is about 0.25 mile (400m) from here.

4 After passing the tearoom, take a left fork, signposted 'kitchen garden', to a pergola. Here are fine views over London, including Canary Wharf and the London Eye. Next take a tarmac path to the right, which passes a metal gate.

5 Turn left, downhill, passing to the left of a lake and keep ahead through woodland. Look out for where you go through a metal gate on the right. Continue along the track ahead, take the next left fork and head uphill. At the next fork take the left-hand path, which then descends.

6 Pass three more ponds to turn sharp right after the last one, along a path to the right of a hedgerow that climbs uphill. At the next junction follow the right-hand path to the top of Parliament Hill where there are more views across London, including this time, St Paul's Cathedral. Continue ahead downhill along a path through the trees and between two ponds before heading uphill again.

7 Keep ahead as the path curves left and then bear right at a path junction, along a path to East Heath Road. Cross over into Devonshire Hill (turn first left into Keats Grove to visit Keats House), and continue ahead, turning right at the crossroads into Rosslyn Hill. Keep ahead uphill to reach Hampstead tube station.

Route facts

DISTANCE/TIME 4.25 miles (6.8km) 2h

MAP OS Explorer 173 North London

START/FINISH Hampstead tube station; grid ref: TQ 264858

PATHS Mainly well-trodden heathland tracks

GETTING TO THE START
Hampstead tube station is on the Northern line. Hampstead lies on the A502 northwest of Camden. There is parking beside the Heath off East Heath Road. This is not in the congestion charging zone.

THE PUB The Flask, 77 Highgate West Hill N6 6BU. Tel: 020 8348 7346; www.fullers.co.uk

KENWOOD HOUSE

MAP REF **TQ271874**

Kenwood House is a hotbed of North London culture. This 17th-century mansion houses one of the best free art collections in the capital, with works by Rembrandt, Reynolds, Turner, Vermeer and Gainsborough all part of the Iveagh bequest (the Earl of Iveagh, better known as brewing boss Edward Cecil Guinness, bought Kenwood House in 1925). As if that wasn't enough, a new addition to the collection is Constable's *Hampstead Heath with Pond and Bathers*. In contrast to the landscapes displayed below, the first floor's Suffolk Collection of paintings consists mainly of portraits by the likes of Van Dyck and Lely. The exterior of Kenwood House was renewed by Robert Adam from 1764 to 1779. Inside he designed some of the house's rooms, such as the stunning library, which has a domed ceiling, rich fabrics and more than enough gilding.

The gardens were the handiwork of Humphrey Repton and are popular with local Londoners. There is woodland, a lake and some trademark Repton features such as ivy-clad shady alleys and carefully crafted panoramas. The gardens have also found favour with wildlife, and four species of bat call them home: it appears that they are not too disturbed by the summer concerts held on the lake.

During the rest of the year there is a packed programme of walks and events, including foraging trips for fungi in the grounds and experience days for those interested in photography, stone carving and other skills. The excellent Brew House Café is famous for its breakfasts, but remains open all day - try the walled garden if there is no space inside.

■ Activity

MUSIC ON A SUMMER EVENING

Kenwood House is a London venue for English Heritage's series of summer concerts, entitled Music on a Summer Evening. Bring a picnic and enjoy the live classical music followed by fireworks. At Kenwood House you can reserve a chair.

■ Activity

CANAL BOAT TRIPS

Several operators run boat trips in restored narrowboats along the Regent's Canal. Departures are from Little Venice or Camden Lock, just beside Camden Market, with boats travelling in either direction. You'll pass through ZSL London Zoo, Regent's Park and the 200-year-old Maida Hill tunnel.

LITTLE VENICE MAP REF **TQ262818**

Little Venice remains one of those lesser-known corners of London that is a pleasant surprise. It doesn't have the most auspicious location - behind Paddington station and within earshot of the Westway flyover - but this triangle of water where the Grand Union Canal meets the Regent's Canal is a peaceful urban oasis. Cream-coloured Georgian mansions surround the waterways, while narrowboats, usually decked in flowers and painstakingly painted, line the canals. Some have been converted into cafés. From here you can take a narrowboat to Camden or walk along the tow path - it will take you about

45 minutes. On the way the style of housing changes from elegant villas to high-rise flats, but the canal is still full of activity, with passing boats, anglers and joggers.

A new initiative called Paddington Waterside is adding residential, commercial and retail space to Little Venice. Eventually Paddington station itself will be connected to the canalside by an underground walkway so many more visitors are expected to discover Little Venice for themselves.

LONDON CANAL MUSEUM
MAP REF TQ304834

A short walk from the grimy King's Cross terminus (walk up York Way, then turn right on to Wharfedale Road), this small museum charts the history of London's network of canals. The canals were essential for trade when Britain went through its convulsive period of industrialisation. Paddington and Camden were linked by canal in 1816 and the British Waterways Agency is reviving much of the network, where it is still above ground. Regent's Canal, which joins the Grand Union Canal at Little Venice, runs 8.5 miles (13.7km) through central London and cost £772,000 to build – twice its original estimate. The London Canal Museum may inspire you to find out more about London's canals but the handsome brick building itself has a few stories. It was built for 19th-century ice cream-maker Carlo Gatti and was the place where he stored ice imported from Scandinavia. During August, the museum hosts special activity days for children.

■ Insight

JUST LIKE THE FILM

The Working Title film *Notting Hill* has a lot to answer for. Residents might be happy about the increase in house prices, but they have had to put up with extra sightseers all keen to see exactly where Hugh Grant's and Julia Roberts' characters conducted their love affair. The bookshop owned by Grant's character is inspired by the shop at 13–15 Blenheim Crescent, while his flat is actually the front of 280 Westbourne Park Road; both streets come off Ladbroke Grove.

■ Activity

NOTTING HILL CARNIVAL

Every August Bank Holiday the smart streets of Notting Hill throb to the rhythms of dub, reggae, samba and calypso as Europe's largest street party parades through West London. The carnival's busiest day is Saturday, while Sunday is traditionally Kids' Day. The popularity of the carnival has spread and visitors from overseas swell the millions who converge on the area. Sound systems are set up on every available corner and stalls sell Caribbean food. The carnival was started in 1959 by West Indian immigrants.

■ Activity

WESTWAY SPORTS CENTRE

London's most extensive indoor climbing walls are at Westway Sports Centre. There are 2,630 square yards (2,200sqm) of climbing with some of the 350 different routes being suitable for beginners and others for experts only. You can also try your hand at bouldering on one of the 50 or so boulder problems at the centre. Tuition, for up to two people at a time, is available, or there are monthly courses for larger groups.

Across Regent's Park

When John Nash designed this area in 1820, it was the grandest piece of town planning ever devised in central London. His scheme was based on a park dotted with villas that looked like separate huge mansions, but which consisted of more than 20 houses. Add to this some grand terraces and the result is idyllic Regent's Park and its little sister, Primrose Hill, from where the views are exhilarating.

Route Directions

1 Take the north exit from Baker Street tube and turn right, along Baker Street.

Cross the road via two sets of pedestrian lights and enter Regent's Park. Turn right.

Cross the bridge over the lake and then bear left, passing the bandstand.

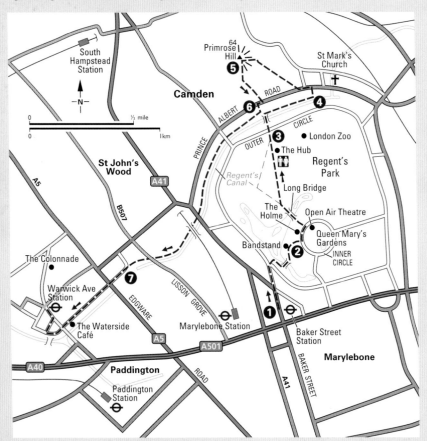

2 Turn left when you reach the Inner Circle road. Beyond The Holme turn left, through the metal gates, and over Long Bridge. When the paths fork ahead, take the right-hand one and keep ahead at the next crossing of paths.

3 Go through the gate, cross the Outer Circle road and follow the path opposite to cross Primrose Hill Bridge. Turn left along a path leading down to the Regent's Canal, then turn sharp left. Continue along this path – which initially leads underneath the bridge and then leads past London Zoo's aviary – for 0.25 mile (400m). You'll also pass under four bridges (some with ornate ironwork) and see some colourful canal boats.

4 At the fourth bridge turn left up the path, signed 'London Zoo, Regent's Park' leading to St Mark's Church. At the gate turn left along Prince Albert Road and past an entrance to London Zoo. Continue for 100yds (91m) then, at the pedestrian lights, cross the road to enter Primrose Hill. Take the right-hand path and follow it uphill to the viewpoint.

5 Follow the path that bears left, leading downhill, to join a straight path that leads to Prince Albert Road. Cross at the zebra crossing and turn right. In about 15yds (14m) turn left.

6 Don't cross the bridge but turn right along a hedge-lined path that bends sharply to the left on to the tow path. Turn right and follow the tow path for 0.5 mile (800m). The banks of the canal are ivy-clad with weeping willows, and palatial homes line this stretch of the walk. Continue ahead under the railway bridges – less enchanting but rest assured that better things lie ahead – and, after a few paces, you'll pass the houseboats moored at Lisson Green before a tow path tunnel.

7 As the canal disappears under another tunnel, walk up the steps on the right and continue along Aberdeen Place. At the end, cross a road and follow Blomfield Road into Little Venice. Cross Warwick Avenue and follow the road as it bends to the right, past the footbridge. Turn right into Warwick Place and left with Warwick Avenue tube 100yds (91m) ahead.

Route facts

DISTANCE/TIME 3.25 miles (5.3km) 1h30

MAP AA Street by Street London

START Baker Street tube station; grid ref: TQ279821

FINISH Warwick Avenue tube station; grid ref: TQ 262821

PATHS Paved streets and tarmac paths

GETTING TO THE START Baker Street tube station is on the Hammersmith & City, Jubilee, Circle and Metropolitan lines. This area is just outside the congestion zone and there are no parking facilities.

THE PUB The Prince Alfred & Formosa Dining Room, 5A Formosa Street W9 1EE Tel: 020 7286 3287; www.theprincealfred.com

❶ Take care with children alongside the canal.

MADAME TUSSAUDS

MAP REF TQ281821

Madame Tussauds waxworks collection is still one of London's most popular attractions, drawing in more than 2 million visitors, despite a rather high entry fee. Famous people know they have made it when their waxwork appears here and, conversely, that their star is shining less brightly when their likeness is melted down to be turned into a more recognisable celebrity.

Madame Marie Tussaud cannot have envisaged how hugely popular her waxworks would become when she started the collection some 200 years ago. Modern techniques and technology mean that some of the newer exhibits are more interactive than others and it may be your only chance to actually touch stars such as J-Lo, Brad Pitt and Robbie Williams. Set pieces include the Garden Party, the Chamber of Horrors, Big Brother, and the Spirit of London, which is a ride through 400 years of the city's history in a black cab.

PORTOBELLO ROAD MARKET   MAP REF TQ817243

Perhaps the world's largest antiques street market and certainly the only one to have a starring role in a film (*Notting Hill*, which starred Hugh Grant and Julia Roberts), Portobello Road Market draws crowds to this west London street when it opens for business on Saturdays. Stalls sell antiques ancient and modern, vintage clothing, maps, suits of armour, curios, jewellery, clothes for men and women, and even food. But a day out here is more about the experience than

picking up a bargain, which can often prove to be elusive as it is not the cheapest market in the city. Leave yourself enough time to make your way through the crowds and keep a look out for a famous face or two among the browsing shoppers, as Notting Hill is now well known as the location of many chi chi celebrity homes.

REGENT'S PARK

MAP REF TQ281829

Regent's Park, originally part of Henry VIII's hunting grounds, is perhaps London's most attractive park. It was landscaped by John Nash in the early 19th century and currently claims London's finest rose gardens, with 400 varieties and 30,000 plants.

The remainder of the 410 acres (166ha) contain 100 acres (40.5ha) of sports pitches and space for activities, including the Lawn Tennis Association accredited Regent's Park Tennis Centre, which has courts available for non-members. There is also a Golf and Tennis School, again with practice facilities available to non-members. Netball players can chose from three courts, while runners have a cinder track on the north side of the park. Football, rugby and hockey pitches are also used by various London schools. The 19 grass softball pitches are also available to the public when the Softball season has finished.

For a more leisurely time, how about rowing in a hired boat on the lake, dodging wildfowl as you go? There are several cafés, including the excellent Garden Café in Queen Mary's Garden.

And if that is too much effort, just sink into a deckchair (summer hire only) and enjoy the genteel surroundings.

SHERLOCK HOLMES MUSEUM MAP REF TQ278821

Although Sherlock Holmes is a fictional character created by Sir Arthur Conan Doyle in the 19th century, he appears to have left many of his personal effects in this museum. His pipe, deerstalker hat and magnifying glass are the key exhibits, but Holmes obsessives may like to peruse the many papers from his case histories as well as the diary meticulously kept by friend, colleague and housemate Dr Watson.

The house, actually 239 Baker Street, has been decorated and organised according to the descriptions in Conan Doyle's books, with Holmes's study on the first floor and Watson's bedroom on the second floor. Actors in costume bring the stories to life.

2 WILLOW ROAD

MAP REF TQ271858

This National Trust house is unique on two counts. First, it is the only Modernist house open to the public in the capital – a fine example from the 1930s. Second, it has rather a surprising James Bond connection. The property was designed by an Austro-Hungarian architect called Erno Goldfinger, who lived in the house until his death in 1987. However, one of Goldfinger's neighbours in Willow Road, Ian Fleming, was so incensed by the demolition of the existing Victorian houses to make way for the block-like construction that he named a villain in

■ Visit

ZSL LONDON ZOO

The zoo is committed to conservation of the world's endangered species and the preservation of fragile habitats – but there's still space for crowd-pleasing favourites such as the giraffes, gorillas and penguins. A new enclosure for the zoo's Western Lowland gorillas, Gorilla Kingdom, allows visitors to enter their forest habitat. Don't overlook the domain of the penguins: the pool, designed by Berthold Lubetkin in the 1930s, is a Modernist architectural classic.

■ Activity

GUIDED WALKS

From April to October, expert National Trust guides from 2 Willow Road escort walkers on architectural tours of London. The walks are themed and include tours of Modernism, Arts and Crafts in Hampstead, Victorian buildings in the City and the Dickensian environs of Southwark. You meet the guide at a pre-arranged spot and booking in advance is essential.

one of his James Bond books after his neighbour. An unimpressed Goldfinger sought legal advice. But he got his own back by designing some of London's most maligned and notorious tower blocks in the 1960s and 1970s, including Trellick Tower in north Kensington.

The house is complemented by an excellent collection of modern art, including works by Bridget Riley, Henry Moore, Max Ernst and Marcel Duchamp. Entry to 2 Willow Road is by guided tour only and opening times are limited. Although booking is not required, it is advisable to arrive early.

■ PLACES OF INTEREST

Camden's Markets
Camden High Street and
Camden Lock NW1 9XJ
Tube: Camden Town.

Fenton House
Windmill Hill NW3 6RT
Tel: 020 7435 3471;
www.nationaltrust.org.uk
Tube: Hampstead.

Freud Museum
20 Maresfield Gardens
NW3 5SX. Tel: 020 7435 2002;
www.freud.org.uk
Tube: Finchley Road.

Hampstead Heath
Hampstead Heath
Information Centre,
Parliament Hill Lido
NW5 1QR. Tel: 020 7332 3322;
www.cityoflondon.gov.uk
Tube: Hampstead.
Rail: Hampstead Heath.

Jewish Museum
129–131 Albert Street
NW1 7NB. Tel: 020 7284 7384;
www.jewishmuseum.org.uk
Tube: Camden Town.

Keats House
Wentworth Place,
Keats Grove NW3 2RR
Tel: 020 7332 3868;
www.cityoflondon.gov.uk/keats
Tube: Hampstead.
Rail: Hampstead Heath.

Kenwood House
Hampstead Lane
NW3 7JR
Tel: 020 8348 1286;
www.english-heritage.org.uk
Tube: Hampstead.

Little Venice
Tube: Warwick Avenue.

London Canal Museum
12–13 New Wharf Road
N1 9RT. Tel: 020 7713 0836;
www.canalmuseum.org.uk
Tube: King's Cross.

Madame Tussauds
Marylebone Road NW1 5LR
Tel: 0871 894 3000;
www.madametussauds.com
Tube: Baker Street.

Portobello Road Market
Market Office, 72 Tavistock
Road W11 1AN
www.portobelloroad.co.uk
Tube: Ladbroke Grove,
Notting Hill.

Regent's Park
NW1 4NR
Tel: 020 7486 7905;
www.royalparks.gov.uk
Tube: Baker Street,
Marylebone, Regent's Park.

Sherlock Holmes Museum
221b Baker Street NW1 6XE.
Tel: 020 7935 8866;
www.sherlock-holmes.co.uk
Tube: Baker Street.

2 Willow Road
NW3 1TH
Tel: 020 7435 6166;
www.nationaltrust.org.uk
Tube: Hampstead.
Rail: Hampstead Heath.

ZLS London Zoo
Regent's Park NW1 4RY
Tel: 020 7722 3333;
www.zls.org
Tube: Baker Street,
Marylebone, Regent's Park.

■ SHOPPING

Books for Cooks
4 Blenheim Crescent
W11 1NN. Tel: 020 7221 1992;
www.booksforcooks.com
Tube: Ladbroke Grove.
Renew your repertoire of
recipes with a cookbook from
this enticing shop.

Diptyque
195 Westbourne Grove
W11 2SB. Tel: 020 7727 8673;
www.diptyqueparis.com
Tube: Notting Hill Gate.
Divine Parisian perfumes,
candles and soaps with
equally gorgeous packaging.

The Dispensary
200 Kensington Park Road
W11 1NR. Tel: 020 7727 8797.
Tube: Ladbroke Grove,
Notting Hill Gate.
Unusual and casual clothing
brands for men and women.

Paul Smith
122 Kensington Park Road
W11 2EP. Tel: 020 7727 3553;
www.paulsmith.co.uk.
Tube: Ladbroke Grove,
Notting Hill Gate.
Quirky men's clothing.

Ray Man
54 Chalk Farm Road
NW1 8AN.
Tel: 020 7692 6261; www.
raymaneasternmusic.com
Tube: Chalk Farm,
Camden Town
Strum a sitar or pluck a
mandolin at this quirky
instrument shop, founded by

Ray Man. Percussion and wind instruments also available.

Rellick
8 Golborne Road W10 5NW.
Tel: 020 8962 0089;
www.rellicklondon.co.uk
Tube: Westbourne Park.
Classic vintage clothing from the 1920s to the 1980s.

Rough Trade
130 Talbot Road W11 1JA.
Tel: 020 7229 8541;
www.roughtrade.com
Tube: Ladbroke Grove.
A legendary independent record label and shop.

Traid
154 Camden High Street
NW1 0NE. Tel: 020 7485 5253;
www.traid.org.uk
Tube: Camden Town
Some donations are recycled and renovated into one-off items. Proceeds go to international development.

■ **PERFORMING ARTS**

Camden Arts Centre
Arkwright Road NW3 6DG
Tel: 020 7472 5500;
www.camdenartscentre.org
Tube: Finchley Road, Hampstead.
Exhibitions, tours, talks and performances.

Canal Café Theatre
Bridge House, Delamere
Terrace, Little Venice
W2 6ND. Tel: 020 7289 6054;
www.canalcafetheatre.com

Tube: Warwick Avenue.
Award-winning comedy and theatre in a small venue.

Electric Ballroom
184 Camden High Street
NW1 8QP. Tel: 020 7485 9006;
www.electricballroom.co.uk
Tube: Camden Town.
Camden's rock showcase.

Electric Cinema
191 Portobello Road
W11 2ED. Tel: 020 7908 9696;
www.the-electric.co.uk
Tube: Notting Hill Gate.
Luxuriously refurbished with a varied programme.

Gate Cinema
87 Notting Hill Gate
W11 3JZ. Tel: 0871 704 2058;
www.picturehouses.co.uk
Tube: Notting Hill Gate.
Leading art-house cinema.

Open-air Theatre
Regent's Park NW1 4NR
Tel: 0844 826 4242;
www.openairtheatre.org
Tube: Baker Street,
Marylebone, Regent's Park.
Shakespeare on a summer evening – book in advance.

■ **SPORT & ACTIVITIES**

Camley Street Natural Park
12 Camley Street N1C 4PW
Tel: 020 7833 2311;
www.wildlondon.org.uk
Tube: King's Cross
A green oasis where you can spot kingfishers and other wildlife. Kids activities available.

London Waterbus Company
Tel: 020 7482 2550;
www.londonwaterbus.com
Companies offering boat trips on Regent's Canal.

Music on a Summer Evening
www.picnicconcerts.com
Concerts at Kenwood House (and other venues) organised by English Heritage.

National Trust
2 Willow Road
Hampstead NW3 1TH
Tel: 020 7435 6166;
www.nationaltrust.org.uk
Tube: Hampstead.
Rail: Hampstead Heath.
From Apr to Oct, expert guides lead architectural tours of London.

Regent's Park Tennis Centre
Tel: 020 7486 4216.
Tube: Baker Street,
Marylebone, Regent's Park.
Open to non-members.

Westway Sports Centre
1 Crowthorne Road W10 6RP.
Tel: 020 8969 0992;
www.westway.org
Tube: Ladbroke Grove,
Latimer Road.
Climbing walls, tennis courts, football pitches and more.

■ **EVENTS**

Notting Hill Carnival
Tube: Notting Hill Gate,
Ladbroke Grove.
The parade on the August Bank Holiday weekend is one of the city's largest festivals.

FLOWER STALL, NOTTING HILL

Carluccio's

32 Rosslyn Hill NW3 1NH
Tel: 020 7794 2184;
www.carluccios.com
Tube: Hampstead

This branch is the outpost of Antonio Carluccio's empire of Italian delicatessen-cafés in London. Located just a short walk away from Hampstead Heath, the menu features salads, antipasti and other light Italian meals.

The Engineer

65 Gloucester Avenue
NW1 8JH
Tel: 020 7722 0950;
www.the-engineer.com
Tube: Chalk Farm

As one of London's earliest gastropubs and with a very attractive Primrose Hill location, the Engineer can be oversubscribed. Like the Lansdowne up the road, it offers a menu that manages to source ingredients from British suppliers where possible for dishes such as roast lamb with wild garlic and spring onions. All the meat is organic.

The Garden Café

Queen Mary's Garden,
Regent's Park NW1 4NU
Tel: 020 7935 5729;
www.thegardencafe.co.uk
Tube: Regent's Park

There are hints of the Garden Café's 1960s origins in the retro furniture, but the menu here is fresh, seasonal and simple. You can choose from snacks and sandwiches or more substantial meals. It's a superb place for lunch or a pre-theatre dinner.

Konstam

2 Acton Street WC1X 9NA
Tel: 020 7833 5040;
www.konstam.co.uk
Tube: King's Cross

The ingredients used in Oliver's Rowe's King's Cross restaurant don't travel far: most have been sourced from within the M25. There's cheese from Norbury, pork from Amersham and chicken from Waltham Abbey. Rowe's reason for this is mainly to reduce food miles but it's also a novel way to get a true taste of London.

The Ledbury

127 Ledbury Road W11 2AQ
Tel: 020 7792 9090;
www.theledbury.com
Tube: Westbourne Park

The Ledbury's austere interior belies the pleasures to be found on its French-influenced menu. The chef, award-winning Australian Brett Graham, delivers intensely flavoured dishes such as roast pigeon with cep and Madeira consommé or fillet of beef with snails, oxtail and celeriac. It's quite expensive, but the two-course lunch is good value.

Queen of Sheba

12 Fortress Road NW5 2EU
Tel: 020 7284 3947;
www.thequeenofsheba.co.uk
Tube: Kentish Town

Popular with North London's Ethiopian community, this local restaurant is an exciting introduction to Ethiopian cuisine. Food is served in the traditional way on *injera*, a thin, stretchy bread. Specials include *bozena shiro*: roast chickpeas and dried meat served with red onion, green pepper, garlic and ginger in a claypot. Don't miss out on the Ethiopian beer and coffee.

The Sea Shell

49–51 Lisson Grove
NW1 6UH
Tel: 020 7224 9000;
www.seashellrestaurant.co.uk
Tube: Marylebone

The Sea Shell has been serving fish and chips for 30 years and has got it down to a fine art. You can get sea bass, sole or salmon, but the traditional option is to order the haddock and chips to take away. The Sea Shell is not far away from Madame Tussauds and Regent's Park.

Day Trips in Outer London

London's transport network – so comprehensive that tube stations can be only a short walk apart – extends well into the suburbs, which means that taking a train out of the city centre for a day couldn't be easier. Head west for genteel Chiswick, or further afield for the must-see gardens and state rooms of Hampton Court Palace, where family activities take place all year round. Alternatively go birding at the Wildfowl and Wetlands Trust Centre at Barnes, spot deer in Richmond Park or life-size model dinosaurs in Crystal Palace Park. Darwin, resident of Down House, would be proud.

CHISWICK HOUSE

CHISWICK HOUSE

Chiswick might be a bourgeois suburb on the Thames, but it does harbour the architectural gem of Chiswick House. The 18th-century Palladian villa was designed by the Earl of Burlington, who wanted to re-create the simple but lavish villas he had seen in Italy. Italianate architecture in London was nothing new, but Chiswick House is a particularly coherent example. There are statues, a temple and cedars in the formal gardens while the understated main building features a central dome and a classical portico supported by six pillars. English Heritage has returned some of William Kent's interiors to their original luxury. Tours are available.

At the end of the gardens, on the Great West Road, detour to Hogarth's House – the summer home used by the artist and engraver William Hogarth. Fine examples of his work, including scenes from *A Harlot's Progress*, *A Rake's Progress* and *Marriage a la Mode*, are exhibited inside. Hogarth is buried nearby at St Nicholas's Church.

CRYSTAL PALACE PARK

Taking its name from the Crystal Palace constructed for the Great Exhibition of 1851, which was transferred here from its original site in Hyde Park, Crystal Palace Park covers the top of one of the highest hills in London. The exhibition centre burned down in 1936, but this small corner of South London has plenty for a day out, as well as some superb views. The park includes both the Crystal Palace Stadium and the Crystal Palace Museum, which describes the Great Exhibition and gives details of the invention of television. But the highlights have to be the park's 33 life-size model dinosaurs. They were moulded in 1854 under the guidance of Professor Richard Owen, a director of the Natural History Museum and the man who coined the word 'dinosaur'. There's also a maze of hornbeam trees, a petting farm and a boating lake.

HAMPTON COURT PALACE

Get set for an action-packed day at one of the grandest royal palaces. Red-brick Hampton Court was built in 1514 by Thomas Wolsey, then Archbishop of York but soon to become Henry VIII's chief minister. By 1528, Henry had relieved Wolsey of ownership. The palace was the scene for many dramas and intrigues during Henry's reign, and all six of his wives spent time here. Queen Victoria opened Hampton Court to the public and it has been a popular attraction ever since. This is partly because of its range of family-friendly events and exhibitions. There are horse-drawn carriage rides in the summer, ghost-hunting tours, Tudor cookery demonstrations and daily tours of the palace with costumed guides. In the winter an ice rink is formed in the west courtyard (book in advance).

It's worth exploring the palace and its gardens regardless of special events. Henry VIII's State Apartments are the centrepiece of the interior, decorated by woodcarver Grinling Gibbons, painter Antonio Verrio and blacksmith Jean Tijou. Outside, try to navigate the famous maze or wander along Chestnut Avenue to admire the Diana Fountain.

Kingston to Hampton Court Palace

This is a traffic-free riverside cycle ride from fashionable Kingston to Hampton Court, the palace that Henry VIII took ten years and spent more than £62,000 (equivalent to £18 million today) to rebuild and extend. Hampton Court Palace dates back to the early 1200s, when the site was occupied by the Knights Hospitallers of St John of Jerusalem. Today the gardens, the palace itself, the world-famous maze and the Great Vine (planted in 1768) continue to attract thousands of visitors a year.

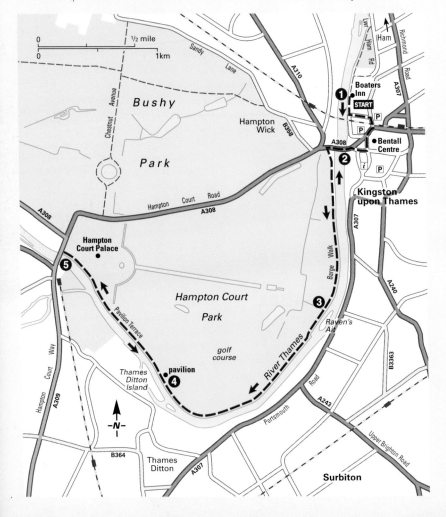

Route Directions

1 From the Boaters Inn, turn south along the shady path by the river. Just before the railway bridge follow the signed cycle route to the left along Down Hall Road. Turn right at Skerne Road and follow the cycle track under the railway bridge. Use the cycle crossing provided to cross Wood Street. Take the buses-and-cyclists-only section of Wood Street along the side of the Bentall Centre, following round to reach the crossroads with Clarence Street. Turn right to approach Kingston Bridge using the clearly marked cycle lane.

2 Cross the bridge on the segregated cycle path and turn left along the riverside. Keep to the surfaced track known as Barge Walk.

3 Soon you reach the yacht club and watersports centre of Raven's Ait (an island in the River Thames). Remain on the riverside path.

4 Thames Ditton Island, with its 48 houses, is the next major landmark on the river. The Pavilion, designed by Sir Christopher Wren, is on the tow path here. When the surfaced track resumes you are now on Pavilion Terrace. Follow the brick wall of Hampton Court Park; soon views of the Broad Walk will emerge. Closer to the palace the path gets wider and will be very busy on sunny summer days so beware of pedestrians and other cyclists on the path.

5 The ride ends at Hampton Court Bridge where you can dismount and explore the palace, gardens and maze before returning to Kingston by the same route.

Route facts

DISTANCE/TIME 7 miles (11.3km) 2h

MAP OS Explorer 161 London South

START/FINISH The Boaters Inn, Kingston upon Thames; grid ref: TQ179702

TRACKS Largely compacted gravel, with some surfaced sections

GETTING TO THE START From Seven Kings car park in Skerne Road go up Down Hall Road, alongside the railway, and head north to The Boaters Inn via the riverside path. The Boaters Inn is in Canbury Gardens, 0.5 mile (800m) north of Kingston Bridge on the eastern bank of the river. Lower Ham Road runs parallel to the A307 Richmond Road. There are pay-and-display car parks in the centre of Kingston.

CYCLE HIRE None available locally

THE PUB The Boaters Inn, Canbury Gardens, Lower Ham Road, Kingston Upon Thames, Surrey KT2 5AU Tel: 020 8541 4672

❶ Give way to pedestrians on the riverside path.

■ Visit

SYON PARK & HOUSE

Syon Park has been the London seat of the Dukes of Northumberland for 400 years. During this time, the family has had its ups and downs: for example, Henry Percy, the ninth Earl of Northumberland, was confined to the Tower of London as he was associated with the Gunpowder Plot. In brighter times, the first Duke, Sir Hugh Smithson, redesigned the estate. He commissioned Lancelot 'Capability' Brown to transform the park, while Italian-influenced architect Robert Adam was charged with injecting some neoclassical flair into the buildings. Visitors can tour some of the rooms, the garden and, best of all, the Great Conservatory.

HORNIMAN MUSEUM

In deepest south London, the Horniman is one of the city's must unsung heroes. The museum reflects the eclectic interests of its founder, Frederick Horniman. It embraces a vast array of objects – musical instruments, jewels, fossils, masks and artworks – that can be loosely described as anthropological. Don't be intimidated: it's a very hands-on place. Outside, the gardens include a medicinal garden with plants from around the world and a nature garden; it's a great place for children to explore. Live world music is performed in the Victorian conservatory.

KEW GARDENS

Even if you're not green-fingered, the Royal Botanic Gardens of Kew, to the west of London on the Thames, are a magical place to spend a day. The gardens were given World Heritage Status in 2003 and have world-class collections of plants displayed in amazing greenhouses, stars themselves.

The Botanic Gardens began as two royal estates. They were combined in 1772 and became a horticultural centre at the time when exotic specimens were brought back from all over the world by sailors, explorers and botanists. That was the science; but there was an art to displaying these plants, for which gardener Lancelot 'Capability' Brown was responsible. In the Western Zone you can see his original design for the Rhododendron Dell. A 656ft (200m) walkway through the treetops of Brown's arboretum was added in 2008. At 59ft (18m) high, it gives you a bird's-eye view.

The gardens cover 300 acres (120ha) so don't expect to see everything in one visit. Highlights include the Palm House, a multi-layered greenhouse designed by Decimus Burton that took four years to construct. On the opposite side of the Palm House lake, Museum No. 1 houses the interactive Plants+People exhibition. In the Pagoda Vista Zone, Burton's Temperate House is the world's largest surviving Victorian greenhouse, home to a Chilean Wine Palm, which is the biggest greenhouse plant in existence, and to the rarest plant at Kew, a cycad from South Africa. And don't miss the Wollemi Pine either, one of the world's rarest trees. Kew has two.

There are plenty of inspiring spots to discover, such as Queen Charlotte's Cottage and Gardens, dedicated to British wildflowers. In winter, London's largest ice rink is here in the gardens.

RICHMOND PARK

Richmond Park is the largest royal park and the most expansive green space in the capital. In the 17th century it was King Charles I's hunting ground, but the 650 deer that roam the park today have little to worry about. As well as 350 fallow deer, there are 300 majestic red deer. The deer herds, which are free to wander the grassland and the rare oak woodlands, are not difficult to spot. Other mammals living in this National Nature Reserve include nine species of bat and there are 144 species of bird, including a growing group of parakeets.

Although the park's landscape has changed very little over the past three centuries, it has a variety of modern uses. Cyclists and runners do laps of the perimeter; you can hire bicycles in the car park at the Roehampton Gate. There are two golf courses and three rugby pitches, which are sometimes used for polo matches. Fishing in the Pen Ponds requires a permit, while power-kiting needs just a good breeze and nerve.

WWT CENTRE

Waders, wagtails and wigeon are some of the bird varieties you may see at the Wildfowl and Wetlands Trust Centre. It is remarkable that such an important habitat for birdlife can be found so close to Europe's largest city and the centre is going from strength to strength. Recent successes include breeding pairs of avocets, an extremely rare wading bird. The centre comprises a man-made wetland that has been a Site of Special Scientific Interest (SSSI) since 2002; the centre itself evolved during the 1990s

▪ Visit

HAM HOUSE

Before stretching your legs in Richmond Park, look around the most complete 17th-century house in Europe, Ham House. The decorative and architectural details, such as tapestries and furniture, have been restored to their original state, while outside the gardens exemplify the English Landscape Movement, which influenced Lancelot 'Capability' Brown. There's a café in the Orangery and the activities include open-air theatre shows, ghost tours and seasonal events.

▪ Visit

TICKETS FOR TENNIS

For two weeks every summer, the nation collectively holds its breath as another plucky British tennis player takes on the world's best in the tournament held at the All England Tennis Club (www.wimbledon.com) in south London. Wimbledon is the only Grand Slam tournament held on grass, although a new, retractable roof for Centre Court will minimise the inevitable disruptions due to rain. A new No. 1 Court stadium has seating for 11,000. Tickets for this spectacle are so sought after that they are allocated by public ballot.

under the guidance of naturalist Sir Peter Scott and opened in 2000. Now, it attracts about 150 species of bird, both permanent residents and those that are simply passing through. Each season there is excitement as a number of different species come and go; check the website for forthcoming arrivals. There's also a full calendar of events, including talks, family walks and children's activities in school holidays.

Richmond Park

Discover London's largest open space. At 2,500 acres (1,010ha) Richmond Park has an abundance of wildlife in its hills, woodland gardens and grasslands, including large numbers of deer. The Isabella Plantation was created from an existing woodland and is organically run, resulting in a rich flora and fauna. More than a thousand species of beetle alone have been recorded in the park, which is a National Nature Reserve and a Site of Special Scientific Interest (SSSI).

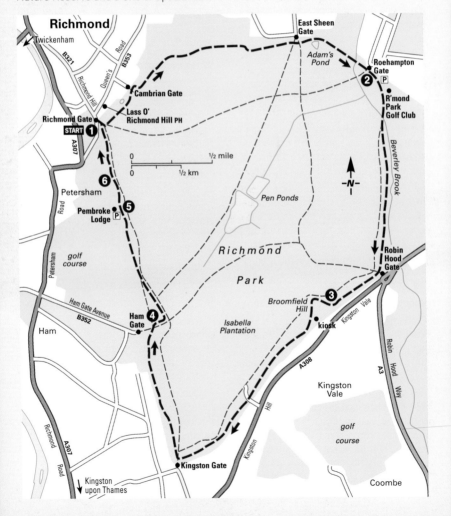

Route Directions

1 On entering the park at Richmond Gate look for the path on the left-hand side. (From Pembroke Lodge car park, return to Richmond Gate and turn right.) The path skirts Bishops Pond. Keep straight on past Cambrian Gate. Adam's Pond is to your right just beyond East Sheen Gate. Sight of the bridge across Beverley Brook means you have nearly reached Roehampton Gate.

2 At Roehampton Gate cross the road. The path continues past the café and car park, where cycle hire is available. The golf course is to your left. Soon the path crosses Beverley Brook once again, then it remains between the brook and the park road as far as Robin Hood Gate.

3 At Broomfield Hill the steepest ascent of the ride awaits; signs advise cyclists to dismount. There is a bench at the top where you can recover, and a refreshment kiosk is just beyond. The Isabella Plantation is to your right. At Kingston Gate the route starts heading north.

4 At Ham Gate the path crosses the road and turns right, ascending parallel to the road. At the T-junction turn left, remaining parallel to the road. Soon the path leaves the road and opens on to a wide tree-lined avenue. As you approach Pembroke Lodge, glorious views of the Thames Valley are unfolding to the left.

5 At Pembroke Lodge the path can become congested with pedestrians. Just beyond the lodge, with the barrow known as King Henry VIII's mound on your left, the cycle path unexpectedly moves to the right. At this point a marker beside the path draws attention to the incredible view of St Paul's Cathedral, 10 miles (16km) away.

6 As you cycle onwards, a panorama of other London landmarks opens out before you. Before long you will be back at Richmond Gate.

Route facts

DISTANCE/TIME 7 miles (11.3km) 1h30

MAP OS Explorer 161 London South

START/FINISH Richmond Gate at Richmond Park; grid ref: TQ184737

TRACKS Largely compacted gravel

GETTING TO THE START Richmond Gate is at the top of Richmond Hill (B321). You can approach from Richmond town centre or, if you are coming from the south, leave the A307 at Star and Garter Hill. There's parking at Pembroke Lodge.

CYCLE HIRE Roehampton Gate, tel: 07050 209249

THE PUB The Lass O'Richmond Hill, 8 Queens Road TW10 6JJ Tel: 020 8940 1306

❶ Some short, steep climbs and a couple of longer ascents through woodland.

■ TOURIST INFORMATION CENTRES

Britain and London Visitor Centre

1 Lower Regent Street
SW1Y 4XT. Tel: 0870 156 6366
Open daily 8–6/6.30.
www.visitlondon.com
This is the official London
tourist office and website.

Local Tourist Information Greenwich (Town) TIC

Pepys House, 2 Cutty Sark
Gardens, Greenwich
SE10 9LW. Tel: 0870 608 2000
Open daily 10–5

Heathrow Airport TIC

Underground Station
Concourse, Middlesex
No phone. Open daily 8–5

King's Cross St Pancras Station TIC

LUL Western Ticket Hall,
Euston Road N1 9AL
No phone. Open Mon–Sat
7.15–9.15, Sun and Bank
Holidays 8.15–8.15

Richmond TIC

Old Town Hall, Whittaker
Avenue, Richmond, Surrey
TW9 1TP. Tel: 020 8940 9125
Open Mon–Sat 10–5, Sun
10.30–1.30

Twickenham TIC

Civic Centre, 44 York Street,
Twickenham, Middlesex
TW1 3BZ. Tel: 020 8891 7272
Open Mon–Fri 9–5

Victoria Station TIC

Opposite Platform 8
SW1V 1JU. No phone.
Open Mon–Sat 7.15–9.15,
Sun and Bank Holidays
8.15–8.15

■ PUBLIC TRANSPORT

Buses

To find out how to get around
London by bus, call London
Transport: 0843 222 1234
(recorded information line);
www.tfl.gov.uk. Daytime
buses in London run Mon–Sat
6am–midnight and Sun
7.30am–11.30pm. Night
buses (the number is
preceded by 'N') run
11pm–6am on main routes;
the majority pass through
Trafalgar Square.

London Underground

The London Underground
system is the oldest and most
extensive of its kind in the
world, with more than 500
trains and over 260 stations.
Trains run from around
5.30am Mon–Sat (7am Sun)
to about midnight Mon–Sat
(11pm Sun).

Travelcards

Travelcards are valid for the
entire transport network in
selected zones, including
buses, tube, Docklands Light
Railway (DLR), Croydon
Tramlink and surburban
national rail services within
the London area. Travelcards
give you unlimited travel
within the zone area paid for,
as well as one-third off most
riverboat services. They are
available from tube stations,
London Travel Information
Centres, national rail stations
in the London area and
newsagents across the
capital. You can buy a
Travelcard up to four days
before you use it. If you're
staying for some time in
London or will be visiting
more than once, a pre-paid
travel pass, called the Oyster
card (www.tfl.gov.uk/oyster,
0845 330 9876), may be
worthwhile. You pay a £3
deposit for the card and
can top it up at stations and
newsagents. Single fares
are generally cheaper with
the Oyster and it can be used
on buses, the Tube and most
trains within the London fare
zones. Just swipe the card
as you pass through the
turnstiles at a station. Check
signs before you board.

■ MAPS

AA Street by Street London

17 maps and atlases in a
variety of sizes, scales and
bindings.

Street by Street A–Z Maps

■ USEFUL WEBSITES

www.visitlondon.com
www.londontown.com
www.english-heritage.org.uk
www.nationaltrust.org.uk
www.tfl.gov.uk

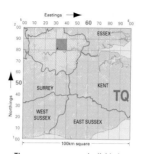

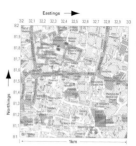

The National Grid system covers Great Britain with an imaginary network of grid squares. Each is 100km square in area and is given a unique alphabetic reference, as shown in the diagram above.

These squares are sub-divided into one hundred 10km squares, identified by vertical lines (eastings) and horizontal lines (northings). The reference for the square a feature is located within is made by combining the numbers of the two lines which cross in the bottom left corner of that square with the alphabetic reference (omiting the small figures). The easting is quoted first. For example, TQ3080.

In this book, we use 6-figure references, which allow us to pinpoint the feature more accurately by dividing the 10km square into one hundred 1km squares (shown on the atlas), and each of these into one hundred 100m squares. These squares are not actually printed on the street atlas but are estimated by eye. The same process is carried out as before, giving an enhanced reference of TQ327811.

Key to Atlas

Primary road single/dual carriageway	Railway & main railway station	Industrial building	Restaurant AA inspected
Primary road service area (Services)	Railway & minor railway station	Leisure building	Hotel AA inspected
A road single/dual carriageway	Underground station	Retail building	Theatre or performing arts centre
B road single/dual carriageway	Light railway & station	Other building	Cinema
Other road single/dual carriageway	County, administrative boundary	Hospital with 24-hour A&E department	Historic house or building
Minor/private road, access may be restricted	River/canal, lake, pier	Post Office	National Trust property
One-way street	Aqueduct, lock, weir	Public library	Museum or art gallery
Pedestrian area	Woodland	Tourist Information Centre	Distillery, brewery or vineyard
Track or footpath	Park	Petrol station, 24 hour Major suppliers only	Monument, statue or other point of interest
Road under construction	Cemetery	Church/chapel	Garden
Road tunnel	Built-up area	Public toilets	Aquarium
Parking		Toilet with disabled facilities	Visitor or heritage centre
Bus/coach station		Public house AA recommended	Abbey, cathedral or priory

The Automobile Association would like to thank the following photographers and companies for their assistance in the preparation of this book. Abbreviations for the picture credits are as follows – (t) top; (b) bottom; (c) centre; (l) left; (r) right; (AA) AA World Travel Library

1 AA/N Setchfield; 4/5 AA/J Tims; 7 AA/N Setchfield; 8t AA/N Setchfield; 8bl AA/S Montgomery; 8br AA/N Setchfield; 9c AA/S McBride; 9b AA/N Setchfield; 10t AA/J Tims; 10c AA/N Setchfield; 10b AA/N Setchfield; 11t AA/J Tims; 11b AA/S McBride; 13 AA/J Tims; 14 AA/J Tims; 18-19 AA/N Setchfield; 21tl AA/J Tims; 21tr AA/N Setchfield; 21b AA/N Setchfield; 22cl AA/N Setchfield; 22cr AA/N Setchfield; 22b AA/T Cohen; 23t AA/N Setchfield; 23b AA/N Setchfield; 25 AA/N Setchfield; 33 AA/B Smith; 37 AA/J Tims; 44-45 AA/P Kenward; 47t AA/R Victor; 47b AA/ N Setchfield; 48cl AA/J Tims; 48cr AA/ N Setchfield; 48b AA/S McBride; 49t AA/N Setchfield; 49b AA/N Setchfield; 56 AA/W Voysey; 62 AA/J Tims; 64-65 Skyscan Photolibrary/Alamy; 67t AA/N Setchfield; 67b AA/N Setchfield; 68c AA/N Setchfield; 68bl AA/N Setchfield; 68br AA/N Setchfield; 69t A Nagahama /Alamy; 69b AA/N Setchfield; 71 AA/M Jourdan; 80 AA/J Tims; 82-83 AA/J Tims; 85 AA/N Setchfield; 86cl AA/C Sawyer; 86cr AA/N Setchfield; 86b AA/R Turpin; 87t AA/M Jourdan; 87b AA/N Setchfield; 89 AA/S McBride; 94 AA/N Setchfield; 98 AA/N Setchfield; 100-101 AA/S Montgomery; 103t AA/N Setchfield; 103b AA/N Setchfield; 104c AA/N Setchfield; 104bl AA/N Setchfield; 104br AA/N Setchfield; 105t AA/N Setchfield; 105b AA/M Taylor; 111 AA/N Setchfield; 116 AA/N Setchfield; 118-119 AA/N Setchfield; 121tl AA/N Setchfield; 121tr AA/N Setchfield; 121b AA/J Tims; 122bl AA/N Setchfield ; 122cr AA/N Setchfield; 122br AA/N Setchfield; 123t AA/N Setchfield; 123b AA/N Setchfield; 136 AA/N Setchfield; 138–139 T French/Alamy; 140 Peter Macdiarmid for Chiswick House/Getty Images.

Every effort has been made to trace the copyright holders, and we apologise in advance for any accidental errors. We would be happy to apply the corrections in the following edition of this publication.